The Mother *and* The Father

Florian Zeller is a French novelist and playwright. He won the prestigious Prix Interallié in 2004 for his third novel, *Fascination of Evil* (*La Fascination du pire*). His plays include *L'Autre*, *Le Manège*, *Si tu mourais*, nominated for a Globe de Cristal, *Elle t'attend* and *La Vérité*. *La Mère* (*The Mother*) received a Molière Award for Best Play in 2011 and *Le Père* (*The Father*) received the Molière Award for Best Play in 2014, starring Robert Hirsch and Isabelle Gelinas (Molière Awards for Best Actor and Actress respectively). It received the Prix du Brigadier in 2015. His last play, *Une Heure de tranquillité* (*A Bit of Peace and Quiet*) opened with Fabrice Luchini, and has since been adapted for the screen, directed by Patrice Leconte. *Le Mensonge* (*The Lie*) will be staged in autumn 2015 with Pierre Arditi and actress wife Evelyne Bouix.

Christopher Hampton was born in the Azores in 1946. He wrote his first play, *When Did You Last See My Mother?*, at the age of eighteen. Since then, his plays have included *The Philanthropist*, *Savages*, *Tales from Hollywood*, *Les Liaisons Dangereuses*, *White Chameleon*, *The Talking Cure* and *Appomattox*. He has translated plays by Ibsen, Molière, von Horváth, Chekhov and Yasmina Reza (including *'Art'*, *Life × 3*, and *The God of Carnage*). His television work includes adaptations of *The History Man* and *Hotel du Lac*. His screenplays include *The Honorary Consul*, *The Good Father*, *Dangerous Liaisons*, *Mary Reilly*, *Total Eclipse*, *The Quiet American*, *Atonement*, *Cheri*, *A Dangerous Method*, *Carrington*, *The Secret Agent* and *Imagining Argentina*, the last three of which he also directed.

also by Christopher Hampton

CHRISTOPHER HAMPTON: PLAYS ONE
(*The Philanthropist*, *Total Eclipse*, *Savages*, *Treats*)

CHRISTOPHER HAMPTON: PLAYS TWO
(*Tales from Hollywood*, *Les Liaisons Dangereuses*, *White Chameleon*, *The Talking Cure*)

APPOMATTOX

screenplays

COLLECTED SCREENPLAYS
(*Dangerous Liaisons*, *Carrington*, *Mary Reilly*, *A Bright Shining Lie*, *The Custom of the Country*)

TOTAL ECLIPSE

THE SECRET AGENT & NOSTROMO

translations

Yasmina Reza's

'ART'

THE UNEXPECTED MAN

CONVERSATIONS AFTER A BURIAL

LIFE X 3

THE GOD OF CARNAGE

Ibsen's

AN ENEMY OF THE PEOPLE

Chekhov's

THE SEAGULL

Ödön von Horváth's

JUDGMENT DAY

also available

HAMPTON ON HAMPTON
edited by Alistair Owen

FLORIAN ZELLER

The Mother

and

The Father

translated by

CHRISTOPHER HAMPTON

FABER & FABER

First published in 2015
by Faber and Faber Limited
The Bindery, 51 Hatton Garden,
London EC1N 8HN

Typeset by Country Setting, Kingsdown, Kent CT14 8ES
Printed in England by CPI Group (UK) Ltd, Croydon, CR0 4YY

A CIP record for this book
is available from the British Library

ISBN 978–0–571–32725–6

Printed and bound in the UK on FSC® certified paper in line with our continuing commitment to ethical business practices, sustainability and the environment.
For further information see faber.co.uk/environmental-policy

THE MOTHER

A BLACK FARCE

The Mother, in this translation by Christopher Hampton, was commissioned by the Ustinov Studio, Theatre Royal Bath, and first presented on 21 May 2015. The cast was as follows:

The Mother (**Anne**) Gina McKee
The Father (**Pierre**) Richard Clothier
The Son (**Nicolas**) William Postlethwaite
The Girl (**Élodie**) Cara Horgan

Director Laurence Boswell
Designer Mark Bailey
Lighting Designer Colin Grenfell
Sound Designer and Composer Jon Nicholls
Movement Director Lucy Cullingford

La Mère in its original French production was first presented at the Théâtre de Paris, Paris, on 4 November 2010.

Characters

The Mother
Anne

The Father
Pierre

The Son
Nicolas

The Girl
Élodie

Act One

SCENE ONE

The Mother and the Father. A soundscape underlining a growing tension and creating a strange atmosphere.

Mother Ah, there you are.

Father Yes.

Mother You're a bit late.

Father A bit, yes. All right?

Mother Yes, yes.

Pause. She resumes, not accusingly.

Where were you?

Father Mm?

Mother This afternoon.

Father What did you say?

Mother Where were you?

Father Why?

Mother Just wondered. That's all.

Pause.

Father What about you? Good day?

Mother Why are you asking me that? When you know the answer.

Father Wanted to know.

Mother You're interested?

Father Yes.

Mother You know perfectly well my day was shitty.

Father (*astonished by her answer*) What's the matter with you? Anne . . .

Mother Nothing. I'm just wondering why you bother to pretend.

Father Me? Pretend what?

Mother To be interested.

Father But I'm not pretending at all, Anne. What are you talking about? I am interested. Very interested.

Mother Well, it's not very interesting. I stayed in, did nothing. Waited.

Pause. The start of a palpable unease.

Your seminar, is it tomorrow?

Father Yes.

Mother You're leaving tomorrow?

Father Yes. In the morning.

Mother Good. Are you happy?

Father It's only a seminar.

Pause.

You seem upset.

Mother No, it's just . . . Nicolas.

Father What?

Mother He still hasn't phoned.

Father Why should he have phoned?

Mother Because I'm his mother. I left him a message, but he hasn't called back. As usual. I don't understand why he never tells me what's happening in his life. Why he never comes by to see me. Never. He behaves as if I didn't exist.

Father He's busy.

Mother Doing what?

Father Mm? I don't know. Living.

She shrugs her shoulders. Pause.

Mother So?

Father What?

Mother Where were you?

Father What do you mean, where was I?

Mother This afternoon.

Father In the office, darling. Why?

Pause. He looks at her, vaguely anxious.

What's the matter with you?

Mother I called the office just now.

Father My office?

Mother Yes. Just now.

Pause.

I wanted to talk to you.

Father Oh, yes?

Mother And they told me you weren't there.

Father When?

Mother This afternoon. They told me you weren't there.

Father I was in a meeting.

Mother Oh, so that's it . . .

Father Yes.

Mother Ah, right.

Father Yes. Didn't my secretary tell you?

Pause. No answer.

Mother (*blandly and lightly, as if she's posing the question for the first time*) Everything all right?

Father Fine . . .

Mother (*still unemphatic*) Where were you this afternoon?

Father Mm? I told you, I was in the office.

Mother You were in a meeting?

Father Yes.

Mother You were preparing tomorrow's seminar?

Father No, no connection.

Mother (*suspiciously*) Really? (*Pause.*) Is it tomorrow, your seminar?

Father You're worrying me, Anne.

Mother I am?

Father Yes. You're weird . . . You are, I promise you, you're weird this evening.

Mother I'm not . . . not at all. What makes you say that? I spend my days on my own bored sick, while you're banging little bitches in hotel rooms, so obviously . . .

Father (*as if he hadn't heard*) Sorry?

Mother Mm?

Father What did you say?

Mother (*as if nothing had been said*) I said I'm aware of a great void.

Father It's your fault as well, you know . . . You don't do anything. You haven't developed any enthusiasms. You stay here, doing nothing. So obviously . . . the world seems . . . dreary to you.

Mother What am I supposed to do?

Father I don't know.

Mother See.

Pause.

Father You have no interests. Since the children left home, it's as if . . . I mean, you have to find yourself something to do. Some focus of interest. Some . . .

Mother I've been had. That's the truth of it. I've been had. All the way down the line.

Father What are you talking about?

Mother There were the children, yes. I took care of them. I certainly took care of the children. Two children, that's quite something. I say two . . . three, including you. Because I took care of you as well. And then I took care of this house.

Father You did.

Mother But now everyone's gone. And here I am on my own. In this big house. Nobody needs me any more. And not even a phone call . . .

Father You're exaggerating . . .

Mother He never phones me. Never. Sara, I'm not saying. But him . . . Nicolas . . . Not even a phone call . . . To ask how I am. To, I don't know, let me hear his voice. He's cut me out of his life.

Father He's in love. It's natural . . .

Brief pause.

Mother (*as if to herself*) Little bitches in hotel rooms . . .

Father You . . . What's the matter with you? Anne . . . Are you all right? You don't look very . . .

Mother (*her tone suddenly completely normal*) I'm fine. What about you? Had a good day?

Father (*disconcerted*) Mm? Yes.

Mother You had meetings?

Father Why are you doing this?

Mother Why am I doing what?

Father You keep repeating yourself.

Mother You didn't have a meeting?

Father I did. I told you I did.

Mother Just one?

Father Yes.

Mother So? Did it go well? Did you close the deal?

Father Mm? Yes.

Mother Great. I'm very happy for you.

Pause.

Father (*walking on eggshells*) And you . . .

Mother Oh, I just stayed here. I didn't do much. Tidied up a bit. Oh, yes, I did go out . . . Did some shopping. I bought a dress. Want me to show it to you? You won't like it, though. It's not your style. It's red. Need some bravado to carry it off. Or else some really important occasion. I'll wear it to your funeral.

Father Have you been drinking today?

Mother Me?

Father Yes. Have you been drinking?

Mother Not a drop.

Father You haven't been drinking?

Mother No. Why are you looking at me like that?

Father No reason.

Pause.

Mother Actually, I should never have had children.

Father What?

Mother I realise now. I should never have had children. Especially with someone like you. Someone who works, I mean. Who has meetings. And seminars.

Father Anne. . .

Mother It's true . . . When we met, I was what, twenty-two? Naive. How could I have known? If you're twenty-two, you have no idea what a huge cheat life is. You don't know anything about it. You can be had so easily. Especially by a man like you. Apparently presentable, superficially at least. Later, as time passes, you find you have to dig a bit deeper. And that's when you find out the extent of the disaster. Anyway, and I don't mean this as a compliment, Pierre, you were a . . . pathetic father. Really. I've been meaning to tell you.

Father Me?

Mother Yes. Pathetic. The complete opposite of a role model. At least for Nicolas.

Father Why are you saying this?

Mother It's what Nicolas told me. He told me he's always taken you as an anti-role model. Obviously, he's an artist. He told me that as far as he was concerned, to be anything like you would mean his life was a failure. To some extent, I agree with him.

Father Are you listening to what you're saying to me?

Anne . . . Are you listening to yourself?

Mother As for Sara . . . Well. She may have admired you a bit. Yes. Vaguely. Until she was nine or ten. You can't blame her for it. After all, you are her father. And then she's not very . . . Not very intelligent, if you think about it.

Father Are you talking about Sara? Are you talking about your daughter?

Mother Oh, don't make that face . . . It's never been a secret. I've always preferred Nicolas . . . Where's the harm in it? But Sara, I don't know . . . (*Whispering, so as not to be overheard.*) I find her unsympathetic. Don't you? Right from the time she was born, really. I noticed right away that she was unsympathetic. It's something physical. Something about her face. Some expression. Don't you think? I remember that first day, yes, the day she was born, I remember feeling strangely repelled.

Pause.

What about you, how was your day?

Father What were you doing while . . .

Mother (*suddenly accusatory*) While *what*?

Brief pause.

(*Playfully.*) I had you there, didn't I? You didn't know what to say . . .

Father I was late back. Is that it? Is that why you're angry with me?

Pause.

Is that why?

Mother Your meeting went on longer than anticipated.

Father Yes. But . . .

Mother So? What's the problem? There is no problem . . . Why do you always make things so complicated? Are you hungry?

Father I've already eaten.

Mother See.

Pause.

Father Listen . . . Seems to me there's something funny going on. You . . . Are you feeling a bit tired? Perhaps I should call a doctor . . .

Mother No, it's just . . .

Father Just what?

Pause.

Mother It's that girl . . .

Father What girl?

Mother You know very well.

Pause.

That girl . . .

Father Who?

Mother Please . . .

Father What?

Mother Stop it . . .

Pause.

Father You mean . . .

Mother Yes.

Pause.

The girl he's in love with.

Father Nicolas?

Mother Yes. D'you think she has something against us? I mean, against me?

Father No, I don't think so. I mean, I've no idea. Why?

Mother It's since he's been seeing her. Before, he used to drop by the house. On Sundays. Not every Sunday, admittedly. But some Sundays. Whereas now . . . I leave him messages, he doesn't even answer.

Father He's growing up.

Mother You call that growing up? I call it being cruel. I hate it.

Father He's twenty-five.

Mother I know he's twenty-five.

Father Sometimes you seem to forget.

Mother How could I possibly forget? Let me remind you I was there the day he was born.

Pause.

No, it's not that. It's something else. I want him to be in love and to live with that . . . *girl*. He does what he likes. It's his life. But that's no reason to forget me. I mean . . . it's ridiculous, but I'm becoming jealous. Can you understand? Jealous of that . . . *girl*. When I'm his mother. It's just incredible. It's incredible. Sometimes I tell myself . . . I should never have had children with a man like you. Cowardice is in the genes. It gets passed on. Like ugliness.

Father Right. Listen . . . I'm going to call a . . .

Mother No.

Father What?

Mother I don't want you to leave me alone.

Father Let me at least fetch you a glass of water.

Pause. He goes out to fetch a glass of water.

Mother I've been thinking about your seminar story, you know. This seminar tomorrow. It is tomorrow morning you're leaving? If you knew how much it makes me laugh. A seminar? I can just imagine you trying to think of some excuse to explain your trips away . . . You really think I'm jealous? I am, but not on your account. He's the one I miss. He's my son. And I'm in the process of losing him. My little darling. My joy. Whereas I've already lost you. Years ago. So go off with your girlfriends . . . Whatever happens, I'm already on my own. I've been had all the way down the line.

He comes back.

Father What were you saying?

Mother I was saying what an arsehole you are.

Pause.

Anyway, you have a good day?

Father (*not knowing what else to do*) Here. Take this.

The Mother drinks.

Mother (*disappointed*) Water?

Father Yes.

Mother Isn't there anything else?

Father No. Better not.

Mother I'd have preferred a . . .

Father I know, but no. It's water.

Pause. She finishes drinking.

Mother Thanks.

Father Better?

Mother All right.

Brief pause.

Father Sure?

Mother Yes, yes.

Father Better?

Mother Yes. Much better.

Brief pause.

Father You ought to go to bed.

Mother I'm not tired.

Father All the same, you ought to go. You ought to take a sleeping pill.

Pause. She takes a deep breath and tries to change the subject.

Mother (*lightly*) What about you? You have a good day?

Father Are you doing this on purpose? Anne, are you doing this on purpose?

Mother What?

Father You've already asked me dozens of times.

Mother Asked you what?

Father Asked me if I've had a good day . . .

Mother Me? Don't talk nonsense.

Pause. She suddenly looks at him suspiciously.

You seem peculiar, Pierre. You do, I promise you. Have you been drinking? Pierre . . . Look me in the eyes . . . Have you been drinking?

Father Look . . .

Mother You have been drinking.

Father What are you playing at?

Mother Me? Nothing. I'm just concerned about you, that's all.

Pause.

By the way, it is tomorrow, your seminar, isn't it?

Father Stop it. Do you hear me? Stop pissing me about.

Pause. Hiatus.

Mother I know very well you're going to end up leaving me. What difference does it make if it's tomorrow or some other day?

Father What are you talking about?

Mother I'm not an idiot. I may seem like one. But I'm not an idiot.

Father What are you talking about?

Mother I know very well you're going to end up leaving me.

Father Are you saying this because of the seminar?

Mother Now the children have gone, there's nothing to keep you here. I know all that.

Father You're talking gibberish.

Mother Stop treating me like an idiot. I know it's your turn. You all leave, one after the other. Having used me up. I'm no use to you any more. You've always told yourself you wouldn't leave, because of the children. Now they're not here any more. So? What are you waiting for? The door's wide open.

Father You're off your head, Anne.

Mother You're finally going to live the life you want to. No need to hide. It's going to be a huge relief to you. A huge relief. No need to invent these seminars for me . . . Or meetings. You'll be able to have it off with your little whores in broad daylight. Fuck them from behind. You know, basically, you're a really horrible man. *I hate to say this*, Pierre.

Father What?

Mother You're a horrible man.

Blackout.

SCENE TWO

Same situation as at the beginning of Scene One. Almost no transition. The actors' tones of voice are neutral and everyday.

Mother Ah, there you are.

Father Yes. I'm a bit late. Didn't you get a message from my secretary?

Mother Yes, I did . . . She told me you had a meeting.

Father Yes.

Mother Did it go well?

Father Yes, yes. We finally closed the deal.

Mother The Markousin deal?

Father Yes. Finally in the bag.

Mother Great. You must be pleased.

Father More exhausted than anything else. What about you? Everything all right?

Mother All right. Nothing special.

Father You stayed in?

Mother Yes. Tidied up a bit.

Father Have you eaten?

Mother Yes. There's some chicken left in the fridge, if you feel like it . . .

Father No, thanks. I'm not really hungry.

Pause.

So you stayed in? I mean, all day?

Mother Mm? Yes. Well, no. I did some shopping. I bought a dress. Guess what colour? Red!

Father Red?

Mother I know. Now I need to find the right occasion to wear it.

Father Are you all right? You seem . . .

Mother What?

Father I don't know. Gloomy. Are you?

Mother No, no.

Pause.

By the way, I meant to tell you . . . I left Nicolas a message. I suggested he come to lunch next Sunday. With . . .

Father With Élodie?

Mother Yes. With her. I'd like it if both of them could come to lunch. Don't you think?

Father What, *this* Sunday?

Mother Yes. It's M—

Father But you know very well I won't be here.

Mother How come?

Father I have this seminar, Anne. I told you about it . . .

Mother The one in Dijon?

Father Yes. I'm leaving in the morning.

Mother But I thought it was . . . It's going on till Sunday?

Father Of course. It lasts four days . . . You couldn't suggest the week after? If not, never mind, do it without me. Except I'd have liked to see them . . .

Mother Anyway, he hasn't even answered. When I leave him messages, it sometimes takes him a week to get back to me.

Father Listen, do what you like. And let me know.

Mother Yes.

Pause.

I don't know why he never calls me back.

Father Nicolas?

Mother Yes. I leave him messages. It sometimes takes him a week to get back to me.

Father It's natural.

Mother You think it's natural?

Father I mean . . . he has his life.

Mother Me too, I have my life. It doesn't stop me thinking about him.

Pause.

Father I expect he'll call you tomorrow.

Mother Yes.

Pause.

What about you? You're leaving tomorrow?

Father Yes. I get a train in the morning.

Mother I'm sure you haven't packed yet.

Father What makes you say that?

Mother I know you. Better than you think. I know you by heart, Pierre. By heart, you know what I mean?

She gazes at him intently, as if, behind this 'I know you by heart', lies the seminar, the afternoons in the hotel, the imminent departure, everything shown in the previous scene which doesn't appear here.

Father What makes you say that in that tone of voice?

Mother Well, I've been married to you for years. You know how long we've been married?

Father Of course I do.

Mother How long?

Father (*playing for time*) Mm?

Mother How long?

Father How long? That's easy . . .

Mother Twenty-five years.

Father Yes. Right. Twenty-five years. Happy years.

Mother In fact, I was thinking about all this just now. About our marriage. Yes. And I was thinking . . . You realise how young I was . . . I was twenty-two. I was Sara's age.

Father Sara's twenty-three.

Mother Mm?

Father I said, Sara's twenty-three.

Mother Yes. Well, that's what I mean, I was younger than she is. I was younger than our children.

Father Yes.

Mother Seems scarcely credible.

Father Yes. It's gone quickly.

Mother Too quickly, you mean. Seems like yesterday.

Brief pause.

Yesterday. And you're leaving tomorrow.

Father I'm not going very far.

Mother Yes, you are. You're going a long way. Much too far. You . . .

Father You think Dijon's a long way?

Mother Mm?

Father You think it's a long way, Dijon?

Mother No. You're right.

Father It's two hours in the train.

She suddenly looks sad. Brief pause.

Mother I hate to say this, Pierre . . .

Father What?

Pause.

What?

Mother No. Nothing.

Blackout.

Act Two

SCENE ONE

The next morning. The Mother is already there. The Father comes in.

Father Up already?

Mother You're very observant this morning. What's the matter with you?

Father Mm? I'm late. I didn't wake up . . .

Mother You're late?

Father Yes. For my train. I'm late. How are you? Sleep well?

Mother No.

Father I heard you last night. You got up, didn't you? Couldn't you sleep?

Mother No. Well, hardly. Does it show?

The Mother is in an obvious state of nervous tension. The Father finishes buttoning up his shirt.

Father Mm? No. But what happened?

Mother He came back.

Father Who?

Mother Nicolas. He's here.

Father Nicolas? Where?

Mother In his room. He's asleep.

Father Oh, yes? What's he doing here? I mean, this wasn't planned . . .

Mother He came back during the night. He's still asleep.

Father Why did he come back? Did he tell you what the matter was?

Mother He didn't tell me anything.

Father He came back during the night?

Mother Yes.

Father And you didn't ask him what the matter was?

Mother I didn't see him. I didn't want to wake him up.

Pause. She prepares breakfast.

Father So why didn't you sleep?

Mother I was . . . I don't know. I woke up during the night. I had an intuition, an intuition that he was here. That he'd come back. So I got up. And went to his room.

Father (*not believing her*) Anne . . .

Mother No. Because this time he was there. I wasn't mistaken this time. He really was there. He was asleep. Fully dressed on his bed. My big boy.

Father Listen . . .

Mother What?

Father Are you sure he's here? I mean, are you sure . . .

Mother But . . . I've just told you . . .

Father Yes, I know.

Mother So? Call me crazy while you're at it.

Pause.

Father I'm going to see him.

Mother No.

Father What?

Mother You'll wake him up. Have your coffee. I'm sure he won't be long.

Pause. He hesitates.

Have your coffee while you're waiting. He'll be down soon. Give him a chance to wake up.

Father You've made some coffee?

Mother Yes. Help yourself. It's all ready.

He hesitates for a moment, then goes and sits down. Pause.

Father You haven't seen my black jacket? I can't find it . . .

Mother It's in the hall, I think.

Father Ah.

Brief pause.

Mother I'll be so happy to see him. Won't you?

Father You speak as if we hadn't seen him for years.

Mother It feels like years.

Father (*once again looking at his watch*) I'm late. I'm really going to have to go.

Mother Yes.

Father My train's in . . . Anyway, I'll have to leave soon.

Mother I know. Yes. To Dijon.

Father I can't understand why I didn't wake up.

Mother I switched off your alarm.

Father What?

Mother I switched off your alarm.

Pause.

Father (*as if nothing had been said*) My alarm. It didn't go off.

Mother Really?

Father No.

Mother (*scarcely concerned*) Ha . . .

Pause. The Father drinks.

Why do you think he's come back?

Father Who?

Mother Nicolas . . . Why has he come back?

Father (*still not believing her*) But Anne . . .

Mother I'm asking you.

Father (*playing along*) How do you expect me to know? I've no idea . . . To see us. To see you.

Mother In the middle of the night? If he wanted to see us, he wouldn't have come in the middle of the night. He knows very well that in the middle of the night, we're asleep. Well, usually.

Father What do you mean?

Mother I'm wondering if . . .

Father If what?

Mother I'm wondering if he hasn't split up with . . .

Father With Élodie?

Mother Yes. With *her*. Don't you think? It's the first thing that came into my head. When I saw him, last night, on his bed. I said to myself, he must have split up with Élodie.

Father D'you think?

Mother I don't know. Maybe. If not, why would he have come back here? I mean, with no warning . . . In the middle of the night.

Brief pause.

Father Maybe you're right.

Mother If that's the case, he'll want to come back and live here . . .

Father There are other possible explanations.

Mother Oh yes? Such as?

Father I don't know. He'll tell us.

Mother I'm sure that must be what it is. He's split up with that . . . girl. Doesn't surprise me. He's much too sensitive to be able to live with a . . . girl like that. Yes. They must have had a row. And he'll be coming back to live here.

Brief pause.

I'm so happy.

Father Anne . . .

Mother You're making a face. As if it were bad news.

Father If he's had a row with Élodie, I don't see how that constitutes good news.

Mother Living with my son again, it's the best thing that could possibly happen to me. Apart from your death.

Father Sorry?

Mother Of course it's good news.

Father What did you say?

Mother It's good news. Who knows what might have happened while you were away for four days?

Father What are you talking about?

Mother I might have felt so lonely that . . . Times like that you don't know what you might do. You could grab a bottle of sleeping pills. For example. You could swallow them with a mixture of other drugs. And then stretch out on a bed. And gently slip away.

Father What are you saying?

Mother I'm saying that now everything's going to be all right. I'm not worried about your going away any more. Because it's true, I was, I was so unhappy you were going off to this seminar. Without me, I mean.

Father (*quite forcefully*) It's a seminar, Anne . . . I'm not going to take you to a seminar. It's a work thing, a seminar. It's not a rest cure. What proves it is it's happening in Dijon. Shit.

Pause.

Mother Sometimes I have dreams about murdering you. They're my favourite dreams. I feel I'm really getting some rest, you see, when I have those dreams. It does me a tremendous amount of good. But I know how to tell the difference between dreams and reality.

Father Anne . . .

Mother I know how to tell the difference, I assure you.

Father Why are you saying this? Mm? So I'll stay?

Pause.

What's all this about drugs?

Mother An idea. That's been floating round my head.

Father Floating round your head?

Mother Yes.

Father Are you saying this to stop me going to my seminar? Is that it? Are you blackmailing me?

Mother (*sincerely*) Would it bother you to get back and find me dead?

Brief pause. No answer.

No, tell me honestly. Would it bother you?

Pause.

Father I'm going to cancel my seminar.

Mother Why? There's no point. Everything's fine.

Father No. Everything is not fine.

Mother I'm telling you, everything's fine. Now that Nicolas is here. Now he's come back. My boy.

Father I'm going to cancel my seminar.

Mother Will you stop using that word!

Father What word?

Mother Will you stop lying all the time!

The Son appears. The Father is very surprised.

Nicolas . . .

Long pause.

Did you sleep well?

The Son goes and sits down in the middle of the room. Pause. Hiatus.

Son Not very.

Mother Would you like some coffee?

Son Please.

The Mother brings him a cup. He's just woken up. Pause.

Sorry to turn up without warning.

Mother Not at all. It's your home. There's no reason to be sorry, my love. Is there?

Father No, of course not.

Mother Your father has to leave. He has a seminar. In Dijon. You think there's such a thing as a seminar in Dijon? Anyway, he has to leave. To get his train. His alarm didn't go off this morning. I switched it off, but he doesn't know about that. I realise it's nothing to be proud of, it was just a small act of revenge. A small act of revenge for all the things he's done to me. Or rather, for all the things he never does to me any more.

Pause. As if nothing has been said.

Would you like some coffee?

Son Please.

Mother Just a minute. There's some in the kitchen. It's all ready.

She goes out. Pause.

Son (*to Father*) You have to go?

Father Yes. Work.

Son Right away?

Father Pretty much. I'm running a bit late.

Son What's the matter with her?

Father She's . . . she's still fragile.

Son I thought things were getting better.

Father Comes and goes, as you know. I'm a bit worried about her at the moment.

Son When are you leaving?

Father Now. I have to go, otherwise I'll miss the train.

Brief pause.

You all right?

Son OK.

Father Nothing serious?

Son No. Nothing serious.

Father You . . . Well, I'd . . . Good of you to drop by. She keeps saying you never come to see her.

Son I know. She leaves me messages.

Pause.

Don't worry. I'll look after her.

Father Yes.

Brief pause.

Good. I'd better go and pack.

Son Have you told her?

Father Mm?

Son Have you told her?

Father No. Not yet.

The Mother comes back.

Mother Here you are, darling. Your coffee.

Son Thanks, Mum.

Mother Would you like something else? Toast? Or something? Would you like me to squeeze you some juice?

Father I'll go and pack.

Mother Right. Yes. Go and pack.

Pause. He leaves.

You don't want anything else?

Son It's nice of you, but no.

Mother Do you believe this stuff about seminars?

The Son shrugs his shoulders.

Not that it matters. How are you?

Son How about you?

Mother I'm all right. I'm happy to see you.

Son Me too.

Mother What's happened? Why have you come back? I mean, just like that, no warning . . .

Son It's tricky.

Mother You don't want to talk about it?

Son No. Not really.

Mother Is it because of her?

Son Mum . . .

Mother Just tell me . . . is it because of her?

Son Yes.

Mother I knew it.

Pause.

Are you unhappy?

The Son makes a face, indicating 'a bit'.

In any case, you know you can stay here as long as you like. You won't get in my way at all.

Son That's good to know.

Mother You can stay here as long as you like.

Son Yes.

Mother Do you think you'll be staying long?

Son I don't know. I'll have to see.

Mother Have you split up?

Pause.

Did she cheat on you?

Son Mm?

Mother Did she cheat on you?

Son What makes you say that?

Mother It's my guess, that's all. I'm sure she slept with another boy and you found out about it. Is that what happened? Bound to be. It's always the same story. She slept with another boy. Not to mention the fact she probably enjoyed it much more than she does with you. Much, much more, it's obvious. I know you must feel humiliated, darling. It's a stab in the heart. No, I understand. Best to put the whole thing behind you, once and for all.

Son I just came back here to sleep, Mum. For one night . . .

Mother But you know, you can stay here as long as you like . . .

Son Yes, you already said that.

Pause.

Mother How did you find out? Did you catch her at it?

Son What?

Mother With the other boy . . . You came home earlier than expected and you found her in another man's arms, is that what happened?

Son We had a row, that's all.

Mother And you walked out of the flat.

Son Yes.

Mother You were right.

Son You never really liked her . . .

Mother Who?

Son Élodie.

Mother I found her vulgar.

Son Élodie?

Mother Yes. And quite ugly. I mean, physically. And she wasn't a nice person. Morally speaking.

He laughs.

What? What are you laughing at?

Son Nothing.

Mother No. Tell me.

Son She didn't like you much either.

Mother Really? Why? Did she say why?

Son She said you were trying to stop me from living. She said –

They're looking each other in the eye. The feeling of an intense confrontation between the Mother and the Son is reinforced by a sound. The Son goes on, deliberately.

– you couldn't live without me. She said I was your breath, your inspiration and that you didn't want to live outside my orbit. She said you wouldn't let me grow up, that you'd rather destroy me than let me grow up away from you. She said you loved me too much.

Pause. Awkward moment.

Mother Honestly, I've no idea where she got all that from.

Pause. They look at one another again.

'Love you too much', it's meaningless. You can't love someone too much. You love them or you don't love them. That's what I think. Don't you? Don't you agree?

The Son smiles.

If that's the sort of thing she said to you, she can't have loved you very much.

Son She loves me. I know she does.

Mother (*sceptically*) She loves you? After what she's done to you? Perhaps I do love you too much, all right, let's admit it, and I hate to say this . . . If she's made you this unhappy, she didn't love you *enough*.

Blackout.

SCENE TWO

Almost immediately. The Mother and the Father are eating their breakfast. The Father is in exactly the same position occupied by the Son at the end of the previous scene.

Father I'm late. It's the alarm. I didn't hear it. I mustn't be long, otherwise I'll miss my train . . . How are you? Sleep well? I heard you last night. You got up, didn't you? Couldn't you sleep?

Mother No. Well, hardly. Does it show?

Suddenly, the Son appears.

Nicolas!

Son Morning.

Mother (*to the Father*) See, I told you he'd be down soon. (*To Son.*) Did you sleep well, darling?

Son Mm? All right.

Brief pause. He goes and sits on the sofa.

What about you, everything all right?

Father You came back last night?

Mother (*annoyed by the Father*) How many times do you need to be told a thing before it sinks in? Come and have some coffee. It'll do you good.

Son Yes, please. Thanks.

Pause.

Mother Your father can't stay.

Father I have to leave. I have a seminar.

Son Oh, yes?

Father Yes.

Son So you're leaving . . .

Father Right away . . . In fact, I'm a bit late. Bad timing.

Mother Off you go, then . . . Otherwise you'll miss your train.

Father Yes. I'd better go and pack.

Son How long are you going for?

Father Four days. A seminar on microcredits.

Mother In Dijon.

Father Yes.

Pause.

Mother Like some more coffee? I'll go and fetch you some. It's all ready. Would you like some more?

Son Please. I've run out.

She goes out. Pause.

You'd better go if you're late.

Father Yes, I'm going.

Pause. He doesn't go.

What about you? You . . . you all right?

Son OK.

Father Nothing serious? You know, I mean . . .

Son What do you mean?

Father Mm? Nothing. So everything's all right . . .

Son Yes. Sorry to turn up without warning . . .

Father No. Not at all. Your mother's happy. She often says she doesn't see enough of you.

Son I know. She leaves me messages.

Father You know, she's often on her own. Since Sara left.

Son She comes back at weekends, doesn't she?

Father Sara? Sometimes. Not very often.

Son And you're here, aren't you?

Father Yes. Yes, I'm here.

Brief pause.

Not always.

Brief pause.

I mean, you know, work.

Pause.

We need to keep an eye on her.

Son Yes.

Father Right. I'm going to finish packing.

The Mother comes back.

Mother Here. Here's your coffee. You used to drink tea in the mornings. Remember?

Son Yes.

Mother You never had coffee. It's since you . . . Anyway, you drink coffee now.

Father I'll be back.

He goes out. Pause.

Mother Would you like something else? Toast or something?

Son It's nice of you, but no. I'm fine.

Mother Sure?

Son Yes.

Mother I got up in the middle of the night. And I saw your jacket in the hall. That's how I . . . Your black jacket. You know, that's how I knew you were here.

Son I meant to warn you, but . . .

Mother There's no need to warn us. It's your house as well.

Pause. The Son drinks his coffee.

I was just thinking about when you were little . . . In the morning I used to get up before you and get your breakfast ready . . . Do you remember? I loved doing that. Putting your little bowls on the table. Heating up the water. Fetching the jam out of the fridge. And then waking you up . . . It was like a ritual, I loved it. Then I used to take you to school . . . Do you remember? I was thinking about it this morning. I just loved that period of my life, you know. I loved it so much. Yes, I think I was really happy in those days.

Pause. The Son is somewhere else. The Mother becomes aware of this.

Anyway, I hope you're all right.

Son OK.

Pause.

Mother You . . .

Son What?

Mother You've had a row, haven't you?

Son Listen . . . I don't much want to talk about it. Sorry. But . . . Well, you understand.

Mother No problem.

Son I . . .

Mother Yes, yes.

Son Sorry, but I . . .

Mother No, no. I understand.

Son Yes, I . . .

Mother In any case, I'm always happy to see you. You're my darling, you know that. And you can always rely on me.

Son Thanks, Mum.

She kisses his hair.

Mother My little boy . . . Do you have clean underwear? Would you like me to do some washing for you?

Son I . . . I don't know. I must have some stuff upstairs.

Mother Not much, I don't think. You took it all with you.

Son Did I?

Mother Yes. But if not, you could always borrow from your father's things in the meantime.

Son We'll see.

Mother Yes. But do you think you'll stay till . . . ? You know Sunday's M—

The Father comes in, talking.

Father Right. Sorry to leave in such a hurry. But I have to go.

Mother Yes, we got that.

Father Yes. Well, I'm off. I'm quite late.

Brief pause.

I'll ring you.

He gets ready to leave. The Son rises to his feet.

Son Are you leaving like that?

Father Like what?

Son Haven't you got something to say?

Pause.

Father (*uncomfortable*) I . . . Well, I'd have to . . . Yes, you mean, to clarify the situation. As regards . . . in fact, the situation is complicated. In the end, the stakes are quite high. Microcredits. But I'll phone when I get there. All right? Right. See you Sunday.

He goes out. Pause.

Mother So there we are, he's gone.

There's a gradual change of mood: the following monologue is spoken in an atmosphere which calls into question how real it might be. Has the Son really come back? Or is all this happening in the Mother's head?

This morning when I told him you were here, that you'd come back during the night, he didn't believe me. I could tell by the way he reacted. He thought I was making the whole thing up to . . . I don't know. To annoy him. I told him you'd come back, you'd come back during the night, and he looked at me coldly. The way you'd look at a madwoman. He must have been saying to himself: she's pretending to be crazy to delay me, to stop me leaving. That's what he was saying to himself. Can you imagine? You should have seen his face . . . You should have seen his face when you walked into the room. He couldn't get over it. He couldn't get over it. Neither could I. I said to myself: here he is, he's back. My darling is back. Mm? You're back. Now tell me you're not going to go away again? Mm? Now you're here, you're not going to go away again?

Brief pause.

You're not answering?

Brief pause.

Why aren't you saying anything? You're not saying anything, but I know what you're thinking.

Suddenly, the Father comes in with his suitcase. A repetition, as if he'd never left. When he speaks, the previous atmosphere returns, with a jolt.

Father Right. Sorry to have to leave in such a hurry.

Mother You finished packing already?

Father Yes. I did it quickly. I didn't want to miss my train.

Pause.

Were you talking to yourself?

Mother Mm? No.

Father You all right?

Mother Yes.

Father You look a bit remote. . .

Mother Me?

Father Yes. What were you thinking about?

Mother Nothing. I was remembering the days when . . . The days when I got up in the morning. I got up to get breakfast ready for you. With the children. Do you remember? Afterwards, I used to take them to school . . .

Father Yes.

Mother You remember? I miss it sometimes.

Father (*tenderly*) Anyway, why don't you try going back to bed? Don't you think? It was nice of you to get up this morning and have breakfast with me, but it's still early. You look exhausted.

Mother You're the one that exhausts me.

Father Mm?

Pause.

Right. Well, I'll ring you when I get there. And take care . . .

Mother Of what?

Father Of yourself.

Brief pause.

Come on . . .

He kisses her and goes out with his suitcase.

See you Sunday.

He smiles at her and leaves. Pause. She smiles at her Son.

Blackout.

Act Three

SCENE ONE

The room, the next day. The Mother has put on her red dress. There's a mirror so that she can look at herself. The Son seems depressed.

Son She still hasn't called.

Mother Have you seen my dress?

Son It's two days now.

Mother You walked out, Nicolas. Be logical. Why are you expecting her to call?

Son I'm not expecting her to. I'm simply remarking that she hasn't called.

Mother Why should she call here? I mean, why *here*? You didn't tell her where you were going.

Son She must suspect I've come back here. Where else could I go? Other than here . . .

Mother Have you seen my dress?

Son Is it new?

Mother Yes. I bought it yesterday. Do you like it? (*She twirls around, innocently.*) Mm? Do you like it?

Son It's . . . red.

Mother You don't like it.

Son Yes, I do. It suits you.

Mother You think so?

Son Yes.

Mother What age do you think I look in this dress?

Son I don't know.

Pause.

Mother How about going out somewhere this evening?

Son Where?

Mother I don't know. Somewhere.

Son To do what?

Mother I don't know. Just to get out.

He shrugs his shoulders.

To get some fresh ideas. Two days now you've been going round in circles.

Son Is that why you put that dress on?

Mother I bought it the other day. For no particular reason. It was the colour I liked. Well? What do you think?

Son I don't really feel like going out is the thing.

Mother It'll do you good.

Son I'm not really in the mood.

Mother That's what I mean.

Pause. She's exuberant.

We could go and eat somewhere. Order shellfish. With a good wine. Don't you think? And afterwards, yes, go out dancing. Get out a bit. Get some fresh ideas.

Son It's nice of you, but I'd rather not.

Mother You never answered me . . . Don't you think this dress makes me look younger?

Son Mum . . .

Mother What? It's just a question.

Son I have no idea.

Mother Just say a number . . . What age do you think I look?

Son I've always been bad with numbers . . .

Mother What do you think people would say, if they saw us arm-in-arm? They wouldn't necessarily think you were my son . . . Maybe they'd say to themselves, look, there she is with her young lover.

Son Stop it.

She moves closer to him.

Mother (*still playfully*) What I'd like to do this evening is go out with my young lover.

Son I told you: I'm not in the mood.

Mother Then what would you like?

Son I'd like you to leave me in peace for a while.

Pause. Her enthusiasm dies away.

Mother Sorry. You're right.

Brief pause. Awkwardness. She falls back into her maternal role.

Would you like me to fix you something to eat?

Son It's nice of you, Mum. But you know . . . I'm not hungry.

Mother Are you still just as unhappy?

Son I'm having trouble breathing, if you really want to know.

Pause.

Mother You've always been like this. So sensitive. Whereas your brothers were always much tougher. Much better equipped for life. They weren't as melancholy as you are.

Son Why are you saying this?

Mother What?

Son I don't have any brothers, Mum.

Mother I know.

Son So? What are you talking about?

Mother I just meant, you've always been different.

Pause.

Son It's not that. It's just that girl meant everything to me. Everything, you know.

Mother But you're the one who walked out.

Son It doesn't make any difference. I couldn't have stayed.

Mother Well, then.

Pause.

Listen, if you like, take a sleeping pill, it'd do you good.

Son A sleeping pill?

Mother Yes.

Son But why?

Mother If you combine it with this little blue pill, look, things will feel much better, you'll see.

Son What is it?

Mother A drug. I take them all the time.

Son To sleep?

Mother No. To stay alive. It'll do you good. Here. Take it.

Son Thanks.

Mother I take them all the time.

Son What are they for? Is it a tranquilliser?

Mother Downer, upper. It's a bit of everything.

The Son accepts the capsule.

I take them all the time.

The Son swallows it.

And now let's try and cheer up. Shall we? We'll . . . I'll take you out to dinner. Grief is the enemy of life.

Son I don't know.

Mother We'll take my car.

Son Are we going far?

She moves closer to him again.

Mother Yes. A very long way.

Son Where?

Mother As far away as possible.

Pause. Suddenly, a young Girl appears: Élodie.

Girl Hello.

Pause. The Son gets up. Something breaks.

Son What are you doing here?

Girl I wanted to see you. (*To the Mother.*) Hello.

Mother Good evening.

Girl Yes. Good evening.

Pause.

I was sure you'd be here.

Son (*hard*) What do you want?

Girl I wanted . . . I don't know . . . to talk to you.

Son What about?

Mother There's nothing to say.

Girl It's so painful. I . . . I don't understand why you walked out like that. So brutally.

Son (*almost aggressively*) You don't understand why?

Girl Well, I do. But it seems so brutal.

Mother You should have thought of that before. It's too late now.

Son Mum.

Mother What?

Pause.

Girl I know I'm not welcome. I accept that it's all my fault. But I couldn't leave it like that without talking to you. I haven't slept for two days.

The Son appears unsettled. Pause.

Aren't you going to say something? Anything . . .

Son No.

The Mother is becoming anxious. A moment of hiatus.

Mother Nicolas . . .

Son What?

Mother Say something.

Son I'm having doubts.

Mother What?

Son I don't know what to do.

The Mother and the Son speak in front of the Girl as if she isn't there or as if she were an inanimate object.

Mother Don't let yourself be taken in, Nicolas. Look at her . . .

Son I am . . .

Mother But look at her properly, Nicolas. They all go through the same routine.

Son (*like a child*) I'm letting myself be taken in, Mum.

It's as if he's under hypnosis.

Mother She comes to look for you, she says two words and you're ready to jump back in?

Son (*who hasn't stopped looking at the Girl*) Yes, but she's beautiful.

Mother Beautiful, beautiful . . . There's no point in exaggerating.

Son Yes, but look at the way she's looking at me.

The Mother moves closer to observe the way the Girl is looking at her Son.

Mother I can't see anything special.

Son You can't see it?

Mother No. She's just a girl looking at you. A girl like any one of dozens in your life.

Son (*a poetic outburst*) It's her rainbow eyes.

Mother Her rainbow eyes? What about her eyes?

Son They bowl me over.

Brief pause. He's still hypnotised. The Mother is getting anxious.

Mother Nicolas, we were supposed to be going out for seafood, just the two of us. We were supposed to be going out dancing. This evening . . . We were going to spend the evening together. Remember? You're not going to cave in, are you? Tell me you're not going to cave in and leave me all on my own.

Girl (*coldly*) Of course he's going to cave in. I'm young and beautiful.

Mother What?

Girl I'm twenty-five years old. I'm young. So's he. We want to live.

Mother What about me?

Girl What about you?

Mother But . . . what's to become of me in all this?

The Girl shrugs her shoulders. Obviously, she couldn't care less.

You make me feel sick.

Girl Here.

Mother What's that?

Girl A handkerchief.

Mother I didn't say I wanted to blow my nose. I said I wanted to throw up. Now, I want to cry. Give me back the handkerchief.

Girl Let yourself go.

Son Yes, let yourself go, Mum.

Pause.

Better?

The Mother shrugs her shoulders.

Girl (*almost impatiently*) Right. Shall we go?

Son Yes. Let's go.

Mother Don't you want something to eat?

Son (*looking at the Girl*) Do you?

Girl (*coldly*) No, thanks. We'd rather go and have dinner in a restaurant.

Mother What kind of restaurant?

Girl (*as if trying to make her salivate*) A seafood restaurant.

Mother With shellfish?

Girl Yes.

Mother And what will you have to drink?

Girl A good wine, I imagine.

Son Yes.

Mother White?

Girl Probably.

Mother What about me? What am I going to do?

Girl You? You'll stay here on your own . . . You'll eat a few biscuits.

Brief pause.

After the restaurant, we're going to make love. We'll go hard at it. It'll be great. He'll have me on the table in the front room and my body will bump against the wooden table and it'll go . . . (*Slowly and sensually.*) Bang . . . bang . . . bang . . . bang.

Brief pause. Awkwardness.

Son Right. We'll be off, Mum.

Girl Yes. We have so many things to say to one another.

Son Yes.

Girl So many things to do.

Son (*laughing*) Yes.

Girl So we'll say goodbye.

Mother You wouldn't like to stay a while longer?

Girl No. It's better if we go now.

Mother I have a bottle of wine . . . Otherwise, I'll only drink it on my own. With all the drugs I'm taking at the moment, I'm a bit scared of mixing . . . Could be dangerous.

Girl Thanks, but we'd rather go.

Brief pause.

Son I . . . Thanks for everything, Mum. Thanks for everything.

Girl Yes, thanks. Do you mind if I call you 'Mum'?

No answer.

Son Right.

Girl Yes. It's late.

Son We'll say goodbye, Mum.

The Mother says nothing.

So, goodbye . . .

Girl Yes. Goodbye, Mum.

The Girl smiles. We need to feel the cruelty of the smile. They leave. The Mother remains on her own for a moment.

SCENE TWO

The Mother pours herself a glass of wine. She drinks it. Slowly. Suddenly, the bell rings. She goes to open the door. The Girl is wearing a red dress.

Girl Hello.

Mother Good evening.

Girl Yes, good evening. I . . . I'm sorry to disturb you . . . I . . . I'm not disturbing you?

No answer. Brief pause. The Girl no longer has the self-confidence of the previous scene.

Am I disturbing you?

Mother Depends what you mean by disturb.

Brief pause.

Girl I . . . I'm looking for Nicolas. I . . . I decided he was bound to be here.

Mother What do you want?

Girl I'd like to talk to him. Is he not here?

No answer.

I decided he was bound to be here with you.

Mother He isn't here.

Girl Really? Didn't he sleep here? I mean . . . Haven't you heard from him? I've been looking for him everywhere.

No answer.

You've no idea where he is?

Mother He's out. I expect he'll be back soon.

Girl I absolutely have to speak to him. Will it disturb you if I wait for him?

Mother Thing is, I have to go out . . .

Girl Oh?

Mother Yes. I have to go out. Shame. Is there something you'd like me to tell him?

Girl Could you ask him to call me?

Mother I'll tell him.

Girl Yes. Please. And tell him it's important. I have to speak to him. One way or another. I have to speak to him.

Mother Yes. I'll tell him.

Pause. She doesn't leave.

Girl Did he tell you? Did he say we'd had a row?

Mother Yes, obviously.

Girl It's so stupid. (*She steps further into the room.*) It doesn't make any sense. I can't understand why he walked out like that. So brutally. You can't smash everything up like that. Without even discussing it.

Mother What do you want, Élodie?

Girl I want . . . him to understand how much he means to me. I didn't sleep all night.

Mother It shows.

Girl Does it?

Mother Yes. You look terrible. If I were you, I'd go to bed.

Girl I won't be able to sleep until I've spoken to him.

Mother I've already told you he's not here.

Girl Then what should I do? Tell me . . . What should I do?

Mother Perhaps you ought to leave him in peace for a while. And change your dress.

Girl My dress? Why? What's wrong with my dress?

Mother It's not really your colour. Red's beautiful, it is, but not on you. I've just bought one myself. Look. It really suits me, don't you think?

Girl Yes.

Mother Makes me look younger, I think.

Girl Perhaps, yes.

Mother We're planning to go out this evening. Get a bit of fresh air. You see, I'd like him to rethink some of his ideas. He's been unhappy for months. Because of you. But things are going to improve now. We're going to be happy.

Pause. The Girl is unsettled.

Girl Do you mind if I smoke?

Mother Sorry?

Girl If I smoke, would you mind?

Mother Yes, I would.

The Girl lights a cigarette. As if to defy her. The Mother watches her lighting it.

It's funny, you remind me of someone.

Girl Who?

Mother Sara.

Girl Sara?

Mother Nicolas's sister. Yes. There's . . . something about your face . . .

Girl Really? I don't know her.

Mother Since she left, we don't see her very often. It's given us a break.

Pause.

Right. I'm sorry, I have to go out.

Girl Yes.

The Mother goes up to her, takes the cigarette out of her mouth and crushes it on the floor.

Mother I don't want to throw you out, but . . . Anyway, I've no idea when he'll get back. Maybe it won't be till late.

The Girl takes an envelope out of her handbag.

Girl Then . . . Could you please give him this?

Mother Mm?

Girl It's a letter.

Mother You want me to give it to him?

Girl Please.

Mother All right.

Girl It's important.

Mother I'll give it to him right away.

Girl And tell him I'll be waiting for his call.

Mother Yes.

Girl It's so stupid. If you knew how angry I was with myself.

Mother If it's any consolation, he's very angry with you too.

The Girl lowers her eyes, disconsolate.

Only this morning he called you a little whore.

Pause. Then, as if nothing had been said:

Right.

Girl Yes, I must go.

Mother Yes. That'd be best.

Girl (*confused*) Sorry. Thank you. Thanks and I'll see you soon.

Mother See you soon . . . Élodie.

Girl And don't forget the letter.

She leaves. Pause. The Mother opens the envelope and begins reading. Then she tears it up.

Blackout.

SCENE THREE

The Mother and the Son are in the same position as at the beginning of Scene One. There's a mirror so that she can look at herself.

Son She still hasn't called.

Mother Have you seen my dress?

Son It's two days now.

Mother Stop rehashing. You've left her. Why are you expecting her to call?

Son I'm not expecting her to. I'm simply remarking that she hasn't called.

Mother Why should she call here? I mean, why *here*? You didn't tell her where you were going.

Son She must suspect I've come back here.

Mother Have you seen my dress?

Son Yes.

Mother I bought it yesterday. Do you like it?

She twirls around, innocently. A repeat of the previous scene.

Mm? Do you like it?

Pause.

How about going out somewhere this evening?

Son Just now . . .

Mother Mm?

Son (*cold and determined*) Just now . . . Yes . . . While I was asleep . . . Someone rang the bell.

Mother Oh?

Son Yes. Someone rang the bell. Who was it?

Mother When?

Son (*cold*) Just now. While I was asleep. Who was it?

Mother Mm? Nobody.

Pause.

Next-door neighbour.

Son Next-door neighbour?

Mother Yes. Why?

Brief pause.

He happened to be passing . . .

Pause. She's uneasy.

So? What do you think? We could go out somewhere. You're not going to tell me you're tired? You've been asleep all day.

Son I would have been asleep all evening as well. Except for that bell ringing.

Mother What bell?

Son (*wanting a confrontation*) The next-door neighbour.

Pause.

Why didn't you give me the letter?

Mother Mm?

Son (*violently*) Why didn't you give me the letter?

Mother What letter?

Pause. Tense moment. She starts again, as if nothing had happened.

We could go out and eat somewhere. Don't you think? And afterwards, yes, go out dancing. Get out a bit. Get some fresh ideas.

Son I'm not in the mood for going out.

Mother I understand. I just suggested it to . . . help you get some fresh ideas.

Son I don't want fresh ideas.

Mother Then what do you want?

Son To be left in peace. To sleep. I'd like to sleep for a week. For a month.

He gets up and heads towards his room.

Mother You're going to bed already?

Son Yes.

Mother You wouldn't like to eat something?

Son I'm not hungry.

Mother Not thirsty? You wouldn't like me to bring you something when you're in bed?

Son No. I just want to sleep. Understand?

He goes out. Pause.

Mother Right. Maybe I'll get breakfast ready for tomorrow morning. I'll get it ready now. I'll put his bowl on the table. Just in case he wakes up very early. That's what I'll do. I'll get his breakfast ready. Just like I used to.

Instead of that, she pours herself another glass of wine. She drinks it. The Father comes in with his suitcase, as if preparing to leave to catch his train. A repetition.

Father Right. I must go. I don't want to be late.

Mother (*getting annoyed*) Honestly, you're really starting to annoy me with these lies! These stories about your seminar! All these stories! Can't you stop treating me like an idiot? Can't you just stop treating me like an idiot the whole time?

Father (*very calm, his tone quite neutral*) Are you sure everything's all right? You seem a bit gloomy today.

Brief pause. Still neutral.

You ought to find yourself a hobby . . . Some focus of interest . . .

Brief pause. Still neutral.

You must be tired, it's early. You ought to go back to bed.

Brief pause.

Right. I'd better go, if I don't want to miss my train.

Mother Fuck you. Piss off! D'you hear me? Piss off!

She throws something at him, which he narrowly avoids. Things speed up.

Father Are you sure everything's all right?

Mother No. No, everything's not all right. Everything's far from all right.

Father What's the matter?

Mother My head is spinning.

He puts down his suitcase.

Father Why would that be?

Mother It's because of the sleeping pills.

Father What? What sleeping pills?

Mother I've taken too many at once. Along with the little blue pills. And now my head feels like it's going to explode. And alcohol. I don't understand what's happening to me.

Father Don't worry. It'll pass.

Mother You think so?

Father Of course.

Mother It's scaring me.

Father No, no . . .

Mother I feel as if I'm about to die.

The doorbell rings.

Father You want me to go?

Mother No. I want you to stay here.

Father I'll go. It's probably the next-door neighbour.

He goes. He opens the door. It's the Girl. The Father speaks to her as if she were someone different.

Oh, it's you.

Girl Are you ready?

Mother Who is it?

Girl (*to the Father*) Is your suitcase packed?

Father It's ready.

Girl (*suggestively*) I hope you haven't forgotten anything.

Father (*smiling*) No.

Girl Have you told her?

Father Mm?

Girl Have you told her?

Father No. Not yet.

Pause.

Good. Shall we go? Just a minute.

He takes a step towards the Mother.

Well, I'm going. I wouldn't want to miss my train. I . . . Do you understand? This seminar is important. It's high stakes for me. I hope you understand. It's a complicated field, the world of microcredits. I can't afford not to go. Mm? Yes. Considering the international . . . economic situation. Yes. So, see you Sunday.

The Girl steps forward on to the stage. She might eventually pick up the cigarette from Act Three, Scene Two, relight it, taking her time, and blow smoke in the Mother's face, as an act of extreme provocation, before saying goodbye to her, as she did in Scene One.

Girl Goodbye, Mum.

Mother Sara . . .

They go out. The Mother puts her head in her hands. Nicolas appears. He has a suitcase in his hand.

What are you doing?

Son (*inscrutable*) What do you think?

Mother Are you leaving?

No answer.

Are you abandoning me? No. Please don't . . . Stay a little longer. Not you . . . Not now.

Son (*inscrutable*) I can't.

Mother Please . . . I'm sorry. I shouldn't have done it. I acknowledge my mistakes.

Son Anyone would think you wanted to stop me from living.

Mother Of course not . . . my little one . . . On the contrary. You know I love you. Stay with me a bit . . . You can go back to her later . . . Stay with me till Sunday. At least till Sunday. You can go back to her later . . . I can't be on my own. Do you understand? I can't be on my own.

The Son crosses the stage. She tries to hold on to him.

Son (*violently*) Stop it!

He breaks away and leaves. She's on her own. She wipes away tears and slowly returns to her task, which is to lay the table for breakfast. Then she crosses to the telephone, dials a number. She gets the voicemail.

Mother Hello, Nicolas, it's Mum . . . I wanted to know if you got my message. My last message. You didn't answer. Why won't you come for lunch here? You could come on Sunday with . . . I mean, you could both come. Well. So think about it and let me know.

Suddenly, the doorbell rings. She gives a start.

Wait, don't go away . . .

She puts down the receiver, not hanging up, and hurries to the door. It's the Girl. She might be wearing a nurse's uniform. Or not.

Girl Am I disturbing you?

Mother Now what do you want? I already told you he's not here.

Girl Sorry?

Mother How many more times do I have to repeat things? He's not here. He's not here. He's not here.

Brief pause.

Girl I'm making a delivery.

Mother What delivery?

Girl (*to others, offstage*) All right. You can come in. (*To the Mother.*) The delivery.

Two Stagehands enter, carrying a white bed, which they proceed to instal in the room.

Mother What's this?

Girl A bed.

Mother Yes. I can see it's a bed. But why are you delivering a bed to my house? I already have one.

Girl It's a hospital bed.

Mother What am I supposed to do with a hospital bed?

Girl You could always get in it.

Mother But I don't want to go to bed.

Girl The sheets are clean.

Mother What difference does that make?

Girl Lie down.

Mother No.

Girl You've taken too many pills. And mixed them with alcohol.

Mother Have I? So? What business is it of yours?

Girl You're starting to feel faint.

Mother What are you talking about? Who asked you to put this bed in my living room?

Girl The next-door neighbour.

Mother What next-door neighbour?

Girl Yours. He found you on the floor. Bit of luck he happened to be passing. Otherwise you could still be there.

Mother Does my husband know what's going on? Where is my husband?

Girl (*checking a form*) He left for the seaside with a young woman. He won't be back till tomorrow. For Mother's Day.

Pause. The Stagehands laugh. She resumes, more conciliatory.

Come along . . . Get into bed.

Mother No.

Girl Please.

Mother I said no.

Girl Don't force me to . . .

Mother To what?

Girl To force you.

Mother Get out of my house!

The Girl makes a sign to the two Stagehands, who approach the Mother. She starts running away from them. They chase her and try to catch her.

No, no! I don't want to!

Girl You'll be much more comfortable. Catch hold of her.

Mother No. No. I want my children! I want my husband! I want my children!

She bursts into tears and lets them put her in the white bed, continuing to speak, but less loudly, almost down to a murmur: 'I want my children. I want my house. I want my husband . . .' As this goes on, the two men tuck her in, while the young woman strokes her face.

Girl (*as if wanting to calm her down*) Shh . . . It's all going to be fine. You'll grow old on your own. Unhappy and alone. Shh . . . No one will care about you. You'll suffer a lot and everything will be as it was. Be calm . . . It'll be very painful, you'll have so much suffering. Shh . . . It's all going to be fine. You'll grow old on your own. Unhappy and alone.

The Girl stands up and goes to hang up the telephone.

Blackout.

Act Four

The Mother is lying down. Beside her, on a chair, the Son is watching over her. Long pause. Then she opens her eyes.

Mother What's going on?

Son Relax.

Mother Where am I?

Son You've been asleep for . . . You took too many sleeping pills, Mum. You've been asleep all day.

Mother But where am I?

Son I'll go and get the nurse. I'll go and tell her you've woken up.

Mother No. Wait. Don't leave me on my own.

Son I'll be back.

Mother No. Stay with me. Just for a minute . . .

Pause.

Son All right?

Mother I'm awake, am I? My eyes are open. Look, my eyes are wide open!

Son Yes, Mum.

Mother That proves I'm awake. Doesn't it?

Son Yes.

Pause.

Mother What am I doing here? Did you bring me? Quick, let's go back home.

Son You have to stay here a while, Mum.

Mother Did you bring me here?

Son You were found stretched out in the living room. Don't you remember?

Mother What? In the living room?

Son A whole bottle. You'd taken a whole bottle . . . After we quarrelled . . .

Mother We quarrelled?

Son Don't you remember?

Mother No.

Pause.

Was it because of the letter? Is that why we quarrelled?

Pause.

I thought you didn't want to hear any more about her, that girl . . .

Brief pause.

Son Are you feeling better?

Mother I don't seem to be able to get up . . .

Son That's normal. You need to wait a bit.

Pause.

Mother Thanks for coming.

Son Did I have a choice?

Pause.

Mother You hate me.

Son I came to tell you I'm going back. To live with her. And that this time you'll have to let go of me.

Pause.

There's no question of your starting in again, do you understand?

Pause.

No question.

Pause. She closes her eyes.

Otherwise, I'll have to . . .

Pause.

Do you understand? I'll have to disappear for good.

Mother And how would that be different?

Son This is the really hard bit.

Mother Is it?

Son Yes.

Mother Why? What's going to happen?

Son (*slowly*) I'm going to hug you. I'm going to hug you very tight.

Mother Yes.

Son And then I'm going to put my hands round your neck.

Mother Oh?

Son (*slowly*) Yes. And then I'm going to squeeze. I'm going to squeeze very tight. And I'm going to look you in the eye. And you're going to look at me. But you won't say anything. You won't even beg for mercy. You'll just let yourself go, it'll be gentle and it'll feel good and you won't say a word and then afterwards everything will be better.

Pause.

Mother Give me a hug, my darling.

He hugs her, then, sticking to his description, he slowly strangles her. She lets it happen. She's smiling. They look at each other, their expressions intense. Then, she fades away.

Pause.

The Father and the Girl appear. The Girl's no longer wearing a nurse's uniform.

Girl Is this it?

Father Yes, this is it. He's done it.

Girl He did it for me.

Father I expect he did.

Girl A beautiful gift. I think he loves me.

Then the Son turns to them. And moves slowly towards the exit. The Father and the Girl, side by side, watch him leave. This time, the Son has his suitcase. He disappears.

Pause.

The Girl rushes after him. The Father remains on his own for a moment. Then he moves towards the bed and sits down to keep watch – it's the same image as at the beginning of the scene, with the Father taking the Son's place. Suddenly, the Mother wakes from her nightmare.

Mother What's going on?

Father Relax.

Mother Where am I?

Father You've been asleep for . . . You took too many sleeping pills, dear. You've been asleep all day.

Mother But where am I?

Father I'll go and get the nurse. I'll go and tell her you've woken up.

Mother No. Wait. Don't leave me on my own.

Father I'll be back.

Mother No. Stay with me.

Pause.

Father Are you feeling better?

Mother What am I doing here? Did you bring me?

Father I made an emergency return.

Mother What emergency?

Father I came back from my seminar, Anne. You were found stretched out in the living room. The next-door neighbour found you on the floor. Luckily he was passing by . . .

Pause.

What happened?

Pause.

It's my fault. I should never have left for that seminar. But you see, it . . .

Mother (*returning to the only subject that interests her*) What about Nicolas?

Father Mm?

Mother Where is he?

Father I left him a message.

Mother He still hasn't called me.

Father No.

Mother Do you think he'll come on Sunday?

Father I'm sure he'll come and see you. Yes.

Mother Did you tell him? Did you tell him I was here?

Father Yes.

Mother (*full of hope*) And what did he say?

The Father doesn't answer. We understand he hasn't yet spoken to him.

Father (*to console her*) He'll come. He'll come and see you.

Mother Do you think so?

Father Of course . . .

Mother No, he won't come. He'll never come.

Father Of course he will . . . Don't worry. I'm sure he'll come on Sunday.

Mother I hope he comes. I left him a message inviting him to lunch. On Sunday. I don't understand why he never tells me what's happening in his life. It's as if he'd disappeared.

Father You know very well, he's busy.

Mother Doing what?

Father I don't know. Living . . .

Pause.

(*In a soothing tone.*) But I left him a message. I'm sure he'll drop by to see you.

Mother You think all sons are like him? I mean, that ungrateful . . .?

Father I suppose it's in the nature of things.

Mother They disappear from our lives, they abandon us without looking back.

Father (*tenderly*) Shh . . .

Mother (*moved*) All that's left to us is the memory of those very early mornings when I had to get up and get their breakfast ready. Yes. The bread and the milk. And then we'd walk to school. Side by side, walking down those streets in the early morning, and I used to carry their little satchels so they didn't get tired. And in front of the school, they'd kiss me so trustingly. So sweetly. Then they'd disappear across the yard. They'd disappear with all the other children. In that crowd of little satchels . . . So tell me . . . What was all that for? Mm? When it comes down to it . . . What was all that for?

Brief pause. The Father doesn't answer.

Father He'll come and see you.

Pause.

He will come.

Pause.

The Son appears (*or not*). *Like an image. The Mother sits up. They look at each other.*

Pause.

Blackout.

THE FATHER

A TRAGIC FARCE

The Father, in this translation by Christopher Hampton, was commissioned by the Ustinov Studio, Theatre Royal Bath, and first presented on 16 October 2014. The cast was as follows:

André Kenneth Cranham
Anne Lia Williams
Pierre Colin Tierney
Laura Jade Williams
Man Brian Doherty
Woman Rebecca Charles

Directed by James Macdonald
Designer Miriam Buether
Lighting Designer Guy Hoare
Sound Designer Christopher Shutt

This production transferred to the Tricycle Theatre, London, on 7 May 2015, with Claire Skinner in the role of Anne and and Jim Sturgeon as the Man.

Le Père in its original French production was first presented at the Théâtre Hébertot, Paris, on 30 September 2012. This production was revived on 17 January 2015.

Characters

Anne

André

Man

Woman

Laura

Pierre

ONE

André's flat.

Anne So? What happened?

André Nothing.

Anne Dad.

André What?

Anne Tell me.

André I just did. Nothing happened.

Anne Nothing happened?

André Nothing at all. Just you bursting in on me as if something had happened, something . . . But nothing happened. Nothing at all.

Anne Nothing happened?

André Nothing.

Anne I've just had her on the phone.

André So? What does that prove?

Anne She left in tears.

André Who?

Anne You can't go on behaving like this.

André It's my flat, isn't it? I mean, this is incredible. I've no idea who she is, this woman. I never asked her for anything.

Anne She's there to help you.

André To help me do what? I don't need her. I don't need anyone.

Anne She told me you'd called her a little bitch. And I don't know what else.

André Me?

Anne Yes.

André Could be. I don't remember.

Anne She was in tears.

André What, just because I called her . . .

Anne No. Because you . . . Apparently you . . .

André Me?

Anne Yes. With a curtain rod.

André With a curtain rod . . . What is this nonsense?

Anne That's what she told me. She told me you threatened her. Physically.

André This woman is raving mad, Anne. With a curtain rod . . . Can you see me doing that? I mean . . . Obviously she has no idea what she's talking about. Physically? With a . . . No, best if she does leave, believe me. She's raving mad. Best if she does leave. Believe me. Especially as . . .

Anne As what?

André Mm? Listen . . . If you must know, I suspect she was . . .

Anne She was?

André She was . . .

Anne She was what?

André (*whispering*) I didn't want to tell you, but I suspect she was . . .

Anne (*impatiently*) She was what, Dad?

André She was stealing from me.

Anne Isabelle? Of course not. What are you talking about?

André I'm telling you. She stole my watch.

Anne Your watch?

André Yes.

Anne Isn't it more likely you just lost it?

André No, no, no. I already had my suspicions. So I set a trap for her. I left my watch somewhere, out in the open, to see if she'd pinch it.

Anne Where? Where did you leave it?

André Mm? Somewhere. Can't remember. All I know is it's now nowhere to be found. Nowhere to be found. I can't find it, there's your proof. That girl stole it from me. I know it. So yes, maybe I called her a . . . Like you say. It's possible. Maybe I got a bit annoyed. All right. If you like. But, really, Anne, a curtain rod, steady on . . . Raving mad, I'm telling you.

Anne sits down. She looks winded.

What's the matter?

Anne I don't know what to do.

André What about?

Anne We have to talk, Dad.

André That's what we're doing, isn't it?

Anne I mean, seriously.

Pause.

This is the third one you've . . .

André I said, I don't need her! I don't need her or anyone else! I can manage very well on my own!

Anne She wasn't easy to find, you know. It's not that easy. I thought she was really good. A lot of good qualities. She . . . And now she doesn't want to work here any more.

André You're not listening to what I'm telling you. That girl stole my watch! My watch, Anne! I've had that watch for years. For ever! It's of sentimental value. It's . . . I'm not going to live with a thief.

Anne (*exhaustedly*) Have you looked in the kitchen cupboard?

André What?

Anne In the kitchen cupboard. Behind the microwave. Where you hide your valuables.

Pause.

André (*horrified*) How do you know?

Anne What?

André How do you know?

Anne I just know, that's all. Have you looked there for your watch?

André Mm? Yes. I . . . I think so.

He frowns.

Anne Dad, you have to understand I can't come every day. It's . . .

André Who's asking you to?

Anne It's the way it is. I can't leave you on your own.

André What are you talking about? You're just being insulting.

Anne No, it's not insulting. You have to accept the idea that you need someone. If only to do your shopping. Not to mention . . . the other stuff. I'm not going to be able to do it any more.

André Have you been in my cupboard?

Anne What?

André Anne. Tell me the truth. Have you been in my cupboard?

Anne No.

André Then how do you know that . . . I mean . . . that I sometimes . . . with my valuables . . . when I . . . Yes. In short. How do you know?

Anne I can't remember. I must have opened it by accident.

André looks appalled. He hurries off towards the kitchen.

Where are you going?

He exits.

I didn't touch anything, Dad. Don't worry. Can you hear me? Dad? I didn't touch anything. (*Almost to herself.*) We can't go on like this. We just can't. Not like this . . . It's impossible . . . Why can't you understand?

He comes back. He's holding his watch.

You found it?

André Found what?

Anne Your watch.

André Oh. Yes.

Anne You realise Isabelle had nothing to do with it.

André Only because I hid it. Luckily. Just in time. Otherwise I'd be here talking to you with no means of knowing what time it was. It's five o'clock, if you're interested. Myself, I am interested. Pardon me for breathing. I need to know exactly where I am during the day. I've always had this watch, you know. If I were to lose it, I'd never recover.

Anne Have you taken your pills?

André Yes. But why are you . . . You keep looking at me as if there was something wrong. Everything's fine, Anne. The world is turning. You've always been like that. A worrier. Even when there's no reason. You're like your mother. Your mother was like that. Always scared. Always looking for reasons to be scared. But that's not the way the world works. All right, fine . . . You'll tell me there's also a kind of . . . That the shadows are closing in. But mostly, *no*. You see what I'm saying? That's what you have to understand. Now your sister, she's always been much more . . . much less . . . She doesn't keep worrying about everything. I mean, she leaves me be. Where is she, by the way?

Anne I'm going to have to move, Dad.

André Move, you mean . . .

Anne Live somewhere else.

André Right. Why not. Sounds good.

Anne I'm going to have to leave Paris.

André Really? Why?

Anne We talked about this. Do you remember?

Brief pause.

André Is that why you're so keen on this nurse living with me? Is that the reason, Anne?

Brief pause.

Well, obviously it is. The rats are leaving the ship.

Anne I won't be here, Dad. You need to understand that.

André You're leaving?

Pause.

But when? I mean . . . why?

Anne I've met somebody.

André You?

Anne Yes.

André You mean . . . a man?

Anne Yes.

André Really?

Anne You needn't sound so surprised.

André No, it's just that . . . since your . . . What was his name?

Anne Antoine.

André That's right. You have to admit, since Antoine, there hasn't been a lot of . . . What's he do, anyway?

Anne He lives in London. I'm going to go and live there.

André What, you? In London? You're not going to do that, are you, Anne? I mean, come off it . . . Never stops raining in London!

Pause.

Do I know him?

Anne Yes. You've met him.

André Are you sure?

Anne Yes, Dad. Lots of times.

André Oh?

Pause. He's trying to remember.

So, if I understand correctly, you're leaving me. Is that it? You're abandoning me . . .

Anne Dad . . .

André What's going to become of me?

Pause.

Why can't he come and live in Paris?

Anne He works over there.

André What about your job?

Anne I can work from home. I don't need to be in Paris.

André I see.

Anne You know, it's important to me. Otherwise, I wouldn't be going. I . . . I really love him.

Pause. He says nothing.

I'll come back and see you often. At weekends. But I can't leave you here all on your own. It's not possible. That's why. If you refuse to have a carer, I'm going to have to . . .

André To what?

Pause.

To what?

Anne You have to understand, Dad.

André You're going to have to what?

She lowers her eyes. Pause.

Anne . . . You're going to have to *what*?

Pause.

Blackout.

TWO

Same room. André is alone.

André I've got to find that lawyer's number. And call him. Yes. I haven't lived all these years to be treated like a . . . like this. No. I've got to phone . . . Yes. A lawyer. My own daughter . . . My own daughter . . .

A Man suddenly appears.

Man Everything all right?

André Sorry?

Man Everything all right?

André What are you doing?

Man Sorry?

André What are you doing here? What are you doing in my flat?

Man André, it's me . . . Pierre.

André What?

Man Don't you recognise me? It's me, Pierre . . .

André Who? What are you doing here?

Man I live here.

André You?

Man Yes.

André You live here?

Man Yes.

André You live in my flat? That's the best yet. What is this nonsense?

Man I'm going to phone Anne.

He moves towards the telephone.

Your daughter . . .

André Thank you, yes, I do know who Anne is! Do you know her?

Brief pause.

You a friend of hers?

No answer.

I'm speaking to you. Do you know Anne?

Man I'm her husband.

André (*caught off guard*) You are?

Man Yes.

André Her husband? But . . . Since when?

Man Coming up for ten years.

He dials a number.

André (*trying to conceal his dismay*) Ah, yes. Of course. Yes, yes. Obviously. Ten years, already? Time passes at such a lick . . . But I thought . . . Didn't you, aren't you separated?

Man Who? Anne and me?

André Yes. You aren't?

Man No.

André Are you sure? I mean, I mean . . . Are you sure?

Man Yes, André.

André But this thing about England? Wasn't she supposed to be going to London to . . . wasn't she?

Man (*on the phone*) Hello, darling. Yes, it's me. Tell me. Will you be done soon? No, no problem. It's just your father isn't feeling very well. I think he'd like to see you. Yes. All right. Fine, we'll wait for you. See you. Yes. Don't be too long. No, no. Lots of love.

He hangs up.

She'll be here soon. She's just out shopping. She's coming straight back.

André She told me she was going to go and live in London. She told me the other day.

Man In London?

André Yes.

Man What was she going to do in London?

André She's met an Englishman.

Man Anne?

André Yes.

Man I don't think so, André.

André Yes, she has. She told me the other day, I'm not an idiot. She told me she was moving. To go and live with him. I even remember telling her it was a stupid idea, because it never stops raining in London. Don't you know about this?

Man No.

André Oops.

Man What?

André Have I put my foot in it?

Brief pause.

(*To himself.*) I've put my foot in it.

Man No, no, don't worry. She hasn't mentioned it to me, but I'm sure she was intending to soon . . .

André You didn't know anything about the Englishman?

Man (*amused*) No.

André Oops-a-daisy . . .

Pause. He puts a hand on the Man's shoulder.

Never mind. Chin up. Anyway, they all end up leaving sooner or later. I speak from experience.

Brief pause.

Man You want something to drink while we're waiting for her? Glass of water? Fruit juice?

André No, but I mean . . . What was I going to say? Oh, yes, that's it, it's come back to me.

Man What?

André It's because of that girl . . .

Man What girl?

André You know, that nurse . . .

Man Laura?

André I've forgotten her name. That girl your wife insists on handing me over to. A nurse. You know about this? As if I wasn't able to manage on my own . . . She told me I needed the help of this . . . When I can manage perfectly well on my own. Even if she had to go abroad. I don't understand why she persists in . . . Look at me. No, take a good look at me . . .

He's trying to remember the name.

Man Pierre.

André That's right, Pierre. Take a good look at me. I can still manage on my own. Don't you think? I'm not completely . . . Mm? You agree? I'm not . . . (*He hunches over like an old man.*) Am I? You agree? Look, I still have the use of my arms, see? (*He illustrates this capability.*) And my legs. And my hands. In fact, it all works wonderfully. You agree? Of course you agree. But her? I don't know where this obsession comes from. This stupid obsession, it's ridiculous. Ridiculous. In truth, she's never known how to evaluate a situation. Never. That's the problem. She's always been that way. Ever since she was little. Thing is, she's not very bright. Not very . . . You agree? Not very intelligent. She gets that from her mother.

Man I think she tries to do the best she can for you, André.

André The best she can, the best she can . . . I never asked her for anything. She's cooking up something against me, I don't know what it is. But she's cooking something up. She's cooking something up, that I do know. I suspect she wants to put me in a home for . . . Yes, she does. For . . . (*He pulls a face representing an old man.*) I've seen the signs. That's what she has at the back of her mind. She almost came out with it the other day. But let me make something absolutely clear: I'm not leaving my flat! I'm not leaving it!

Man This isn't your flat, André.

André Sorry?

Man If you remember, you moved here, I mean you moved to our place while you were waiting for . . .

André What?

Man Yes. While you were waiting for a new carer to be found . . . Because you quarrelled with the last one . . . With Isabelle.

André Did I?

Man Yes. Don't you remember? That's why you're staying in our place. While you wait.

Pause. André looks slightly lost.

André So, Antoine . . .

Man Pierre.

André Yes. So you're telling me, I'm in your place?

Man Yes.

André laughs and rolls his eyes.

André Now I've heard everything.

The door opens. A Woman enters carrying a shopping bag. It's not Anne.

Woman There, I was as quick as I could be. Everything all right? What's happening?

Man Nothing much. Your father seemed a bit confused. I think he wanted to . . . Didn't you? Wanted to see you.

Woman Something wrong? Are you all right, Dad?

He doesn't recognise her.

Dad?

André I . . .

Woman Yes?

André What is this nonsense?

Woman What are you talking about?

André Where's Anne?

Woman Sorry?

André Anne. Where is she?

Woman I'm here, Dad, I'm here.

She realises he doesn't recognise her. She looks anxiously at the Man.

I went to do some shopping. And now I'm back. I'm here, everything's all right.

André I . . . I see . . . But . . . What did you buy?

Woman A chicken. Sound good? Are you hungry?

André Why not?

He seems lost. And gloomy.

Man Look, let me have it. I'll go and fix everything.

Woman Thanks.

He takes the bag and steps out into the kitchen. Pause.

Pierre called me. He said you weren't feeling very well?

André I feel fine. Except . . . There's something that doesn't make sense . . . About all this, I mean.

Woman What?

André It's difficult to explain. It's difficult. You wouldn't understand.

Woman Try me.

André No!

Pause.

Woman You look worried.

André Me?

Woman Yes. You look worried. Is everything all right?

André Everything's fine. It's just . . .

Woman Just what?

André (*annoyed*) I was just sitting there. Sitting quietly in the drawing room looking for a telephone number, and suddenly your husband arrived and . . .

Woman Who?

André Your husband.

Woman What husband?

André Mm? Well, yours, my dear. Not mine.

Woman Antoine?

André Your husband.

Woman Dad, I'm not married.

André Sorry?

Woman I got divorced more than five years ago. Have you forgotten?

André What? Well, then, who's he?

Woman Who?

André Are you doing this on purpose? I'm talking about . . . him. Who just left with the chicken.

Woman The chicken? What are you on about, Dad?

André Right here, just a minute ago. Did you not hand over a chicken to someone?

Clearly she doesn't know what he's talking about.

The chicken! A minute ago, you were holding a chicken, were you not? A chicken. A *chicken*!

Woman What chicken? What are you talking about, Dad?

André I'm worried about you, Anne.

Woman Me?

André Yes, believe me, I'm worried about you. Don't you remember? She doesn't remember. Are you having memory lapses or what? You'd better go and see someone, old girl. I'm talking about something that happened not two minutes ago. I could have timed it.

He checks his watch is still on his wrist. He's relieved.

Not two minutes ago. Yes. I could have timed it. With a chicken for dinner. Which you'd bought.

He approaches the kitchen.

Woman I think you're mistaken, Dad. There's no one in the kitchen.

André Well, that's very peculiar! He was there two minutes ago.

Woman Who?

He goes out for a minute.

Dad . . .

He comes back.

André He's vanished.

He looks around everywhere.

He must be hiding somewhere.

Woman (*smiling*) The man with the chicken?

André Your husband. Why are you smiling? Why are you smiling?

Woman Nothing. Sorry.

André All this nonsense is driving me crazy.

Woman Calm down.

André You want me to calm down?

Woman Yes. Come over here.

André There's something funny going on. Believe me, Anne, there's something funny going on!

Woman Come and sit down next to me. Come on . . .

He goes to sit down on the sofa. He's upset. The Woman smiles at him and rests a hand on his.

Now don't worry. Everything'll sort itself out. Mm?

André I don't know.

Woman (*tenderly*) Yes, it will. Don't worry. Have you taken your pills?

André What's that got to do with anything?

Woman Let's give you your pills. The evening dose. Then you'll feel better.

André It's been going on for some time. Strange things going on around us. Haven't you noticed? There was this man claiming this wasn't my flat. A really unsympathetic-looking man. A bit like your husband. Only worse. In my flat, you understand what I'm saying? It's the best yet. Don't you think? In my flat. He told me . . . But . . . This is my flat, isn't it? Mm? Anne . . . This is my flat?

She smiles at him without answering. She prepares his medication.

Isn't it?

Brief pause.

Tell me, Anne, this really is my flat, isn't it?

Pause. She hands him his medication. In silence.

Blackout.

THREE

Simultaneously, the same room and a different room. Some furniture has disappeared: as the scenes proceed, the set sheds certain elements, until it becomes an empty, neutral space. Anne is alone in the room. She's on the phone.

Anne No, I'm expecting her any minute. I know. I hope things will work out this time. Yes. You can't imagine how . . . difficult it is sometimes. The other day, he didn't even recognise me. I know. I know. Lucky you were there. Yes. Yes. No, I can't see any other solution.

Suddenly, the bell rings.

Ah, there's the bell. Yes. Must be her. Yes. I . . . I'll say goodbye. All right. Lots of love. Me too. Me too.

She hangs up. She's on her way to answer the bell. The door opens: it's Laura.

Hello.

Laura Hello. Not too late, am I?

Anne No, no. Not at all. Come in. Come in.

Laura enters.

Laura Thanks.

Anne I was expecting you. Come in. Thanks for coming today.

Laura That's OK.

Anne My father's in his room. I . . . I'll go and fetch him. Would you like something to drink?

Laura No, thanks.

Anne Make yourself comfortable. I . . . So, yes, as I was telling you, I . . . He's a bit upset by the whole idea of . . .

Laura That's OK.

Anne Yes. And that can cause him to . . . Anyway, I think he's a bit annoyed with me. I'm telling you this just to warn you he's capable of reacting . . . unexpectedly.

Laura Has he lived on his own up to now?

Anne Yes. In a flat, not too far from here. It worked. I was able to look in on him practically every day. But eventually, we've had to come to another arrangement. It wasn't viable any more.

Laura I understand.

Anne He had several carers one after the other. But he had difficulty getting on with them. He has his ways . . . He can be quite eccentric. Yes. Quite eccentric. That's why I moved him here, in with me. I thought it'd be better for him. But I can't manage him on my own. It's too much for me. And I have to work. I have to . . . Yes. That's why I . . . Well, that's why I need someone to help me.

The door to the inner room opens. André appears. He's in his pyjamas.

André Did I hear the bell?

Anne You did . . . Dad, I'd like you to meet Laura.

Laura How do you do, sir.

Anne I explained to you that Laura was going to come by today so you could meet.

André Hello.

Laura Hello.

André You're . . . gorgeous.

Laura Thank you.

André But I . . . Do we know each other? We do know each other, don't we?

Laura No, I don't think so.

André Are you positive?

Laura Yes, I think so.

André Your face is familiar.

Laura Is it?

André Yes. Sure? I have a definite impression I've seen you before.

Laura Maybe. I don't know.

Anne Well. So, Laura's come by to see us to get a bit of an idea of how you live and to see to what extent she might be able to help you.

André I know, dear, I know that. You've already told me a hundred times. (*To Laura.*) My daughter has a tendency to repeat herself. You know what it's like . . . It's an age thing. Would you like something to drink?

Laura You're very kind, but no thanks.

André Sure? An aperitif? Must be about time for an aperitif, isn't it? What time is it? It's . . . Where's my . . .? My . . . Wait a minute . . . My . . . Hang on, I'll be right back.

He moves towards the kitchen and exits.

Anne He's going to look for his watch.

Laura Oh?

Anne Yes. He's a very . . . punctual man. Even if he is in his pyjamas in the middle of the afternoon.

Laura Perhaps he's been having a siesta.

Anne (*a little embarrassed*) I expect so. Yes.

Pause.

Laura In any case, he's charming.

Anne Yes. Not always. But most of the time, yes, he's charming. Like I said, he has his ways.

Laura Well, that's good.

André returns, wearing his watch.

André Just as I was saying, time for an aperitif. I have two watches. I've always had two. One on my wrist and the other in my head. It's always been that way. Would you like something, young lady?

Anne Dad . . .

André What? I'm allowed to offer our guest something, aren't I? What would you like?

Laura What are you going to have?

André A small whisky.

Laura All right, I'll take the same.

André Excellent. So, two whiskys. Two! I'm not offering you one, Anne. (*To Laura.*) She never drinks alcohol. Never.

Anne It's true.

André Never. Not a drop. That's why she seems so . . .

Anne So what?

André Sober. Her mother was the same. Her mother was the . . . soberest woman I've ever met. Whereas her little sister . . . It was quite another story.

Laura You have two daughters?

André That's right. Even though I hardly ever hear from the other one. Elise. All the same, she was always my favourite.

Pause.

Do you ever hear from her? I don't understand why she never gets in touch. Never. Dazzling girl. A painter. An artist. Here's your whisky.

Laura Thank you.

André Cheers.

They clink glasses.

I'd give everything I own for a glass of whisky. Don't you think?

Laura Well, I don't own all that much . . .

André Don't you? What do you do for a living?

Laura Well, I . . . I look after . . . other people.

André Other people?

Laura Yes. My job is to help people who need help.

André (*to Anne*) Sounds like one of those girls you're always trying to dump off on me.

Pause.

Must be a difficult job, isn't it? Spending all day with some . . . (*He makes a face signifying an invalid.*) Am I right? I couldn't stand it.

Laura What about you, what did you do for a living?

André I was a dancer.

Laura Were you?

André Yes.

Anne Dad . . .

André What?

Anne You were an engineer.

André What do you know about it? (*To Laura.*) Tap dancing was my speciality.

Laura Really!

André You seem surprised.

Laura (*laughing*) Yes, a little bit.

André Why? Can't you imagine me as a tap dancer?

Laura Of course. It's just . . . I've always loved tap dancing.

André You as well? I'm still great at it. I'll give you a demonstration one day.

Laura I'd love that.

He gets up, takes a few hopeless steps. Laura starts laughing. He stops.

André Why are you laughing?

Laura (*still laughing*) It's nothing. Sorry. Sorry.

André starts laughing as well.

André You don't believe me?

Laura Of course I do. It's just . . .

André Just what?

Laura Just . . . the whisky.

André That's it, I know. I know who you remind me of. I know who she reminds me of.

Anne Who?

André Elise. That's right. Elise, when she was her age.

Laura Elise?

André My other daughter. The younger one. She's an angel. Don't you think?

Anne I don't know.

André Yes. There's a resemblance.

Anne Maybe. Slightly.

André There's a resemblance. Yes.

Laura There is?

André Yes. Your habit of . . . That unbearable habit of laughing inanely.

Everyone stops laughing. Pause.

I had you there, didn't I? Ha ha.

Brief pause.

That's the way I am. I like taking people by surprise. It's a special brand of humour.

Brief pause.

(*Suddenly serious.*) You see, the situation's very simple. I've been living in this flat . . . oh, for a long time now. I'm extremely attached to it. I bought it more than thirty years ago. Can you imagine? You weren't even born. It's a big flat. Very nice. Very big. And I've been very happy here. Anyway. My daughter is very interested in it.

Anne What are you talking about?

André Let me explain the situation. My daughter is of the opinion that I can't manage on my own. So she's moved in with me. Ostensibly to help me. With this man she met not long ago, just after her divorce, who has a very bad influence on her, I have to tell you.

Anne Look, what are you talking about, Dad?

André And now she'd like to convince me that I can't manage on my own. The next stage will be to send me away I don't know where . . . Although, in fact, I do know where. *I know*. Obviously, it'll be a much more efficient way of getting hold of my flat.

Anne Dad . . .

André But it's not going to happen that way. I may as well tell you. I have no intention of leaving any time soon. No, you heard me. I intend to outlive you. Both of you. That's right. To outlive both of you. Yes. Well, I don't know about you . . . But my daughter, definitely. I shall make a point of it. *I'm* going to inherit from *her*. Not the other way round. The day of her funeral, I shall give a little speech to remind everyone how heartless and manipulative she was.

Anne I'm very sorry about this.

André Why? She understands completely. You're the one who doesn't understand. (*To Laura.*) I've been trying to explain to her for months that I can manage very well on my own. But she refuses to listen. Refuses. So since you're here and your job consists of 'helping people', perhaps you can help me to explain things clearly to her: I don't need any help from anyone and I will not leave this flat. All I want is for people to bugger off and leave me in peace. If you'd have the kindness to explain that to her, I'd be most grateful to you. There we are.

He empties his glass, gets up, brings a note out of his pocket and throws it down on the table, as if he's paying the bill.

Having said that, it was a great pleasure, I'll be leaving you.

He exits.

Laura When you said he had his ways, you weren't kidding . . .

Anne No . . . I'm very sorry.

Anne seems particularly upset.

Laura Don't be. That sort of reaction is quite normal.

Anne No, I'm very sorry.

Laura It'll all turn out fine. I'm certain of it. Don't worry.

Brief pause.

It'll all turn out fine.

Anne You think so?

Pause. Laura drinks a mouthful of whisky.

Blackout.

FOUR

Anne is alone. Nevertheless, she speaks as if she's talking to someone, as if she's undergoing cross-examination.

Anne I couldn't get to sleep. I was so tired, so tired that falling asleep was beyond me. So I got up. And I went into his room. Dad's room. He was asleep. He looked like a child. His mouth was open. He was at peace. So peaceful. And I don't know what came over me, a kind of wave of hatred, and I put my hands around his throat. Gently. I could feel his pulse beneath my hands. Like little butterflies. And then I squeezed. My hands. Squeezed them very hard.. He didn't open his eyes. He didn't close his mouth. It was just living through one bad moment. One minute. Hardly that. One bad moment. Still. But it was curiously gentle. Gentle and still . . . When I relaxed the pressure, when I took my hands away, I sensed he was no longer breathing, that it was over at last. It was as if the butterflies had flown. Yes. He had a slight smile. He was dead. He was dead, but I had the impression he was thanking me.

Pause.

Blackout.

FIVE

Anne is laying the table for dinner, while Pierre is reading the newspaper. The chicken is cooking in the kitchen.

Anne No, it went well. I think. She said she'd start tomorrow.

Pierre Here?

Anne Yes.

Pierre Good.

Anne Yes. Then we'll see how the first day goes. I was so afraid it wasn't going to work. But in the end it was fine. He was charming.

Pierre There you are, you see.

Anne Yes. She seems very sweet. Very competent. He turned on the charm for her . . .

Pierre Oh, yes?

Anne Yes. You should have seen it . . . He told her he'd been a dancer. A tap dancer.

Pierre (*smiling*) No . . .

Anne Yes. She started to laugh. Not in a mocking way, you understand. There was something kind about her.

I was relieved. I don't know how to describe it to you. As if she was going to be able to . . . Well, as if the two of them were going to get on really well . . .

Brief pause.

He said she reminded him of Elise.

Pierre Oh, yes? But how old is she?

Anne I don't know. Thirty. Something like that.

Pierre Is she pretty?

Anne Why? Are you interested?

Pause.

Pierre What's the matter with you?

Anne With me?

Pierre Yes. You seem odd. If it went well, that's good news, isn't it?

Anne Yes, yes.

Pierre So? What's the matter with you? Tell me.

Anne It's just . . .

Pierre What?

Anne Just now . . . When he didn't recognise me . . . When I went down to buy the dinner . . . I . . . I don't know. It did something to me.

Pierre I understand.

Anne I'm finding it so hard.

Pierre Come. Let me give you a hug.

Anne I saw it in his eyes. He didn't recognise me. Not at all. I was like a stranger to him.

Pierre You have to get used to it.

Anne I can't manage to.

Pierre I think you can, I think you're managing very well.

Anne You're wrong. Sometimes I think I'll never manage to. And he keeps talking about Elise. I don't know what to say to him when he starts. I'm lost.

Pierre Come here . . .

Brief pause.

Anne I had a terrible nightmare last night. I dreamt I was strangling him.

Pause. She pulls herself together.

Did you put the chicken in the oven?

Pierre Yes. It'll be ready in . . . in ten minutes. Hungry?

Anne No.

Pause. She smiles at him.

Had a good day?

André comes in. He sees Pierre. He doesn't recognise him. He frowns.

Dinner'll be ready in ten minutes, Dad. That suit you?

André Very good, dear. Suits me fine. Suits me . . . But . . . Hello.

Pierre smiles at him distractedly.

Anne You hungry, Dad?

André Yes, yes. But . . . We have guests this evening?

Anne No. Why?

André Nothing, nothing . . .

André stares at Pierre. Pause.

Pierre (*to Anne*) Nothing special. Few meetings. Nothing special. Still waiting for Simon's answer. Always takes longer than you expect. Hopefully they'll sign before the end of the month. What about you?

Anne I told you. Laura came by. Didn't she, Dad? Laura came to see us just now.

André Who?

Anne Laura. The young woman who came to see us just now.

André Oh, yes.

Anne And then I've been here ever since.

Pierre Didn't do any work?

Anne Not really. I've been with Dad.

André Has anybody seen my watch? Can't seem to find it.

Anne Again?

André I've been looking for it for some time.

Anne You must have put it in your cupboard. Don't you think? In your hiding-place . . .

André starts, afraid that Pierre has heard the word 'cupboard' and will discover his hiding-place.

André (*intending this for Pierre*) What are you talking about, Anne? I really don't know what you're talking about. What cupboard? Mm? There's no cupboard. No cupboard. No. I don't know what you're talking about. (*To Anne, almost a whisper.*) Couldn't you be more discreet?

Anne (*speaking more quietly*) Have you looked in your cupboard?

André I've just come from there. It's not there. I must have lost it somewhere. Or else it's been stolen.

Anne No, it hasn't.

André (*getting annoyed, but still whispering*) What do you mean, 'No, it hasn't'? The watch must be somewhere! It can't have flown away! So why do you say 'No, it hasn't'? Why do you say that, when it very well might have been stolen? My watch.

Anne You want me to go and look?

André Very much so. If it's not a bother. Because it's a worry. I'm worried. I'm losing all my things, everyone's just helping themselves. If this goes on much longer, I'll be stark naked. Stark naked. And I won't even know what time it is.

Anne I'll be back.

She exits. Pause. Pierre is reading his paper. André watches him from across the room. He clears his throat to get his attention, as one might with someone one doesn't know.

André Her-hum . . .

No reaction from Pierre.

Her-hum . . .

No reaction. André clears his throat even more forcefully. Pierre looks up.

Am I disturbing you?

Pierre Sorry?

André I'm not disturbing you?

Pierre Mm? No.

Pause. Pierre returns to his paper.

André Might you have the time?

Pierre Yes.

André Ah. Thanks.

Brief pause. Pierre continues to read the paper.

So what time is it? Exactly.

Pierre looks at his watch.

Pierre Almost eight.

André That late? Shouldn't we be sitting down to dinner . . .?

Pierre Yes. As soon as the chicken's ready. In ten minutes.

André We're having chicken this evening?

Pierre Yes. The one Anne just bought.

André It's pretty, your watch. It's . . . It's pretty. It's . . . Is it yours? I mean, is it yours?

Pierre Mm? Yes.

André May I see it?

Pause. Pierre looks up from the paper.

Pierre So. Apparently it went very well?

André Yes, very well. What?

Pierre Well, your meeting with . . . the carer.

André Oh. Yes. Very well. Very well. She's very . . .

Pierre Apparently she looks like Elise.

André Is that right?

Pierre I've no idea. I've never seen her.

André (*still focusing on Pierre's watch*) No, it . . . it went well. Anne seemed pleased. You know, it's mainly for her. I don't really need . . . I mean, it's mainly for Anne. Might I have a look at it? Your watch . . .

Pierre You're right, it's important for her that this works out. She's been worried about you, you know. It makes her very unhappy when you fall out with . . . Anyway, let's hope everything works out this time. Mm? That you'll be happy with this woman. That you'll welcome her a little more . . . warmly. What is it about my watch?

André Nothing. I was just looking . . . I wanted to check if . . . It's pretty. Very pretty. Did you buy it?

Pierre Sorry?

André No, I mean . . . Was it a present or did you buy it?

Pierre I bought it. Why?

André I don't suppose you kept the receipt . . .

Pierre What are you talking about?

André For your watch.

Pause.

Pierre I was talking about Anne.

André Do you know her? I mean, you . . . Yes, that's right, you're her . . . Aren't you? You're her . . .

Brief pause.

I'm her father. Nice to meet you. I expect we'll see a bit of each other. If you're her new . . . I mean, if it lasts. As for me, I can't explain why. We never really hit it off.

Pierre moves away from him.

Pierre Why are you saying that?

André Just telling you. We never really got on. Not like Elise. My other daughter. Now she, she was marvellous.

But I haven't seen her for months. She's travelling, I think. She's going round the world. She's been very successful, I can't blame her. Painter. She's a painter. So, obviously. But I'd be so happy if she came to see me one day. I'd take her in my arms and we'd be glued to one another for hours on end, like we used to be a long time ago, when she was little and she still used to call me 'little daddy', 'little daddy'. That's what she used to call me. Nice, isn't it, 'little daddy'?

Pause. Pierre starts slowly moving towards André.

Pierre Can I ask you a guestion?

André Yes.

Pierre gets closer to him. There's something threatening about his approach.

Pierre But I want an honest answer. Nothing fancy . . . Can you do that for me?

André (*caught off guard*) Yes.

Pierre Well, then . . .

Brief pause.

How much longer do you intend to hang around getting on everybody's tits?

Pause.

Blackout.

SIX

Anne and André. Earlier in the day.

Anne I need to talk to you, Dad.

André Good start.

Anne Why do you say that?

André My dear, when someone says 'I need to talk to you', it means they've got something disagreeable to say. Don't you find?

Anne No. Not necessarily.

Brief pause.

André So? What was it you wanted to say?

Anne (*calculating that this might not be a good time*) Never mind. Nothing.

Pause.

I've spoken to Pierre.

André Pierre?

Anne Pierre, Dad. I've spoken to him.

André Your husband?

Anne Dad . . . Pierre isn't my husband. I'm divorced.

André Make your mind up.

Anne I divorced Antoine five years ago. I now live with Pierre. He's the man I'm living with.

André I don't care for him, that fellow. He's unsympathetic.

Brief pause.

Don't you think? I don't care for him.

Anne He's not a fellow, Dad. He's the man I love.

Pause.

Anyway. I've spoken to him and . . . You remember at first, when you came to our place, it was . . . I mean, it was a temporary solution. You remember? It was . . . a stop gap. Because you'd fallen out with Isabelle. But . . .

How shall I put this? I'm wondering if it wouldn't be better to . . . You're comfortable in your room, aren't you?

Brief pause.

You're comfortable in that room at the back?

André Yes.

Anne Yes, you seem to be comfortable there. That's what I thought. And I was wondering if it wouldn't be more reassuring . . . Nicer for you if we came to a joint decision that you should move in here. I mean, for good. With us. On condition we get someone to help us.

Brief pause.

That way, we could see each other every day. It'd be easier. What do you think?

Pause.

I've spoken to Pierre about it. He agrees.

André But . . . I thought . . . I thought you were going to go and live in London.

Anne No, Dad. Why do you keep going on about London? I'm staying in Paris.

André I don't understand any of this nonsense. You keep changing your mind. How do you expect people to keep up?

Anne But there was never any question of going to London, Dad.

André Yes, there was. You told me.

Anne I didn't . . .

André I'm sorry, Anne. You told me the other day. Have you forgotten?

Pause.

You've forgotten. Listen, Anne, I have a feeling you sometimes suffer from memory loss. You do, I'm telling you. It's worrying me. Haven't you noticed?

Anne In any event, I'm not going to London.

André Good thing too. It never stops raining in London.

Anne I'm staying here. So's Pierre.

André What about me?

Anne You as well, Dad. You're staying here.

André What about your sister? Where's she?

Anne Dad . . .

André What?

Brief pause.

If you knew how much I missed her . . .

Pause.

Blackout.

SEVEN

A little later in the evening. Anne and Pierre are at the table. André is standing in the doorway to the kitchen. Anne and Pierre haven't noticed him.

Pierre He's *ill*, Anne. He's ill.

Anne and Pierre simultaneously realise that André is in the room. Anne starts. Feeling of awkwardness.

Anne Dad. What are you doing, standing there? Come and sit down. Come on.

He doesn't respond.

Dad . . .

Pause.

Come on, Dad.

Pause.

Come and sit down.

Pause.

Blackout.

EIGHT

Lights up almost immediately. Anne, Pierre and André. A few minutes earlier in the evening. They're eating.

Pierre So it went well?

Anne Yes. It went very well. Don't you agree, Dad?

André What?

Anne It went well, your meeting with Laura . . .

André Yes.

Anne You made her laugh a lot.

André Did I?

Anne Yes. She thought you were charming. So she told me. She told me she thought you were charming. That you had your ways, but that you were charming. Those are the words she used. She's coming back tomorrow morning. To start working here.

Brief pause.

Like a bit more?

André I would. It's good, this chicken. Don't you think? Where'd you buy it?

Anne Downstairs.

André Oh?

Anne Why?

André No reason. It's good.

Anne Pierre?

Pierre No, thanks.

He pours himself another glass of wine.

Is she doing full days? I mean . . .

Anne Yes. Till six.

Pierre And then?

Anne What d'you mean?

Pierre After six.

Anne I'll be there.

Pause.

Pierre (*to André, like a criticism*) Are you satisfied?

André What about?

Pierre You have a daughter who looks after you properly. Don't you? You're lucky.

André You're lucky too.

Pierre You think so?

Pause. Anne gets up and takes the chicken into the kitchen.

André What's the matter with her?

Pierre Anne? She's tired. Needs a bit of sun.

André You need to look after her, old man. Why don't you go away somewhere?

Pierre Why? You want me to tell you why?

Brief pause.

Sometimes I wonder if you're doing it on purpose.

André Doing what?

Pierre Nothing.

He pours himself another glass.

We had planned to go to Corsica ten days ago.

André Oh?

Anne comes back.

Pierre Yes. But we had to cancel it at the last minute. Do you know why?

André No.

Pierre Because of your row with Isabelle.

André Isabelle?

Pierre The woman who was looking after you. Before Laura. Have you forgotten?

Brief pause.

We weren't able to go and leave you on your own in Paris. We had to cancel our holiday and bring you over here. And now it seems you're going to stay here. For good. If I understand correctly.

Pause.

(*To Anne.*) He's forgotten . . . Amazing.

Anne Stop it.

Pierre What?

Anne You're being a bit . . .

Pierre A bit what?

Anne Sarcastic.

Pierre Not at all, Anne. I think I'm being very patient. Very patient. Believe me.

Anne What are you trying to say?

Pierre Nothing.

Anne Yes, you are. Tell me.

Pause.

Why are you telling me how patient you are?

Pierre I think anyone but me . . .

Anne Yes?

Pierre Anyone else would have pressured you to . . .

Anne To what?

Pierre To do what the situation calls for, Anne. What it calls for.

Anne And that is?

Pierre You know very well.

Pause.

André Where's the chicken? Did you take the chicken away?

Anne Yes. Did you want some more?

André Yes. Is it in the kitchen?

Anne I'll go and fetch it for you.

André No, it's all right, I'll go.

He gets up and goes into the kitchen. Pierre pours himself another glass of wine.

Anne Why do you say things like that in front of him?

Pierre What did I say?

Pause.

Anyway, he forgets everything.

Anne That's no reason.

Pause.

Pierre Listen . . . I totally understand your feelings.

Anne No, you don't understand.

Pierre I do . . . What I don't understand is . . . I mean, you do so much for him. I respect you for that. You took the decision to bring him here. And why not? But . . . How can I put this? I honestly think you ought to come up with a different solution . . . He's completely lost it, Anne.

Anne Don't talk like that.

Pierre How do you want me to talk? I'm telling the truth. We have to find another arrangement.

Anne Such as?

André appears in the doorway. He listens to the conversation. Neither of them has noticed him.

Pierre Putting him in an institution.

Anne A home?

Pierre Yes. A nursing home.

Pause.

It'd be better for him.

Anne Why are you saying this to me today? I mean, when tomorrow morning . . . There's this . . .

Pierre Yes. You're right. We'll see. Maybe it'll work very well with this girl. You seem to think she's good. But believe me, the moment will come when . . . However good she is . . . He's *ill*, Anne. He's ill.

Anne and Pierre simultaneously realise that André is in the room. Anne starts. Feeling of awkwardness. A repeat.

Anne Dad. What are you doing, standing there? Come and sit down. Come on.

He doesn't respond.

Dad . . .

Pause.

Come on, Dad.

Pause.

Come and sit down.

He leaves without saying anything, as if he's going to bed.

Pause.

Blackout.

NINE

The room, a little later. Pierre is alone. Anne appears in the doorway.

Pierre Is he asleep?

Anne Yes. Finally.

Pierre What a day . . .

Anne Yes.

Pause.

Pierre All right?

Anne (*not altogether there*) He asked me to sing him a lullaby. Can you believe it? He asked me . . . He wanted a song. He closed his eyes right away and went to sleep. With his mouth open. He looked peaceful. So peaceful.

Brief pause.

Pierre Did he hear? I mean . . .

Anne Yes. You saw. He was there. Yes. He couldn't help hearing.

Pierre But he didn't say anything?

Anne No. He looked so sad. He was like a little boy. I told you, he asked me to sing him a lullaby. Brought tears to my eyes.

Pierre I'm sure.

Anne I remembered what sort of a man he was . . . I was scared of him when I was little. If you only knew. He had so much authority. And now he's here, I sing him a lullaby and he goes to sleep. I can hardly believe it. It's sad. Terribly sad.

Brief pause. She looks at Pierre's wine glass.

Any left?

Pierre Yes. Want a glass?

Anne Please.

He gets up and pours one for her.

He was so strange this evening.

Pierre You know what I think.

Anne It's worrying me.

Pierre Shall we change the subject?

Anne Yes. Sorry.

Long pause. Sense of strain.

It's good, this wine.

Pierre Yes.

Pause. They smile at each other. Silence. Have they nothing else to say to one another?

Anne I've been thinking about what you said earlier on. About . . . When you said we should put him in a nursing home . . .

Pierre Oh?

Anne Yes. And I was thinking maybe you were right. Maybe you were right after all.

She empties her glass in one go. Pierre smiles at her.

Blackout.

TEN

Still the same room, which is continuing to shed various elements. André comes out of the kitchen. Morning. He's carrying a cup of coffee.

André Did I sleep well? Did I sleep well? How should I know? I suppose so. Ah. I've forgotten the sugar. Sugar!

Woman's Voice (*from the kitchen*) I'll bring it.

André Yes. To put in the . . . I always take sugar in my coffee. In the mornings. I take two sugars in my coffee. It's easy, men fall into two groups. Those who take sugar in their coffee and the rest. The whole battle is to know which category you belong to. Personally, I belong to the category of those who take sugar. In their . . . Sorry, but that's the way I am. Right. Are you bringing the sugar?

Woman's Voice (*from the kitchen*) Yes, yes, on my way . . .

André I certainly didn't sleep well. I had a nightmare. This man turned up in my flat. I banged straight into him and he claimed it was his place. He claimed he was your husband or something along those lines. He threatened me.

He suddenly becomes aware of a new piece of furniture, one he doesn't recognise.

What's this? Who put this here? Anne? But . . . Anne? You might at least consult me before you . . . Anne?

Laura comes in.

Laura Here. I brought you the sugar.

André is surprised to see her.

André What?

Laura You take two?

André Where's Anne?

Laura She went out.

André Really? Already?

Laura Yes.

André What time is it?

Laura She'll be back soon. At the end of the day. I'm going to look for your medication.

André No. Wait.

Laura What?

Brief pause. He's reluctant to let her know how surprised he is.

I'll be back. I'm just going to look for your medication.

She exits. He seems troubled by her presence.

André I've lost my watch again. Shit. Honestly. I . . . I . . . I should have got dressed before she arrived . . . I'm not very presentable. In my pyjamas.

Laura returns with a glass of water.

What time is it?

Laura Time for your medication. Here we are. Best to take them now. Then it's done. Don't you think? There are three today. This little blue one . . . That's the one you like. Your little blue pill. Pretty colour, isn't it?

André Can I ask you a question?

Laura Yes.

André Are you a nun?

Laura No.

André Then why are you speaking to me as if I were retarded?

Laura Me?

André Yes.

Laura But I'm not speaking to you as if you were . . . Not at all, I . . .

André (*imitating her*) 'Your little blue pill.' 'Your little blue pill.'

Laura I'm sorry. I didn't think you . . .

André It's really unpleasant. You'll see when you get to my age. Which'll happen sooner than you think, by the way. It's really unpleasant.

Laura I apologise. I . . . It won't happen again.

André (*imitating her*) 'Your little blue pill.'

She hands him the glass of water.

Have you noticed anything?

Laura What about?

André What do you think? About the flat!

Laura No. What about it?

André It's changed.

Laura You think so?

André Yes. This piece of furniture, for instance. There. Who put that there?

Laura I don't know. Your daughter, I imagine.

André Obviously. My daughter . . . Obviously . . . All the same, it's extraordinary! Not even to ask my opinion. I . . . Do you know what's being planned? For this flat?

Laura No.

André I do. I keep my eyes open. I keep my ears open. I know everything.

Pause.

By the way, I wanted to apologise if I was a little . . . Last time we met . . . Yes, maybe I said a bit . . . too much . . . Or maybe not enough . . . Don't you think?

Laura No problem. Your daughter warned me. She told me you had your ways.

André Oh?

Laura (*benevolently*) Yes. And you know what my answer was?

André No . . .

Laura I said 'Pleased to hear it'.

André Did you? That's nice. You look so like Elise, it's amazing. My other daughter. Not Anne, no. The other one. The one I love.

Laura Anne told me what happened to her. I'm sorry. I didn't know.

André Didn't know about what?

Laura Her accident.

André What accident?

Laura What?

André What are you talking about?

Laura (*hesitantly*) Nothing . . .

Pause.

Are you taking your medication? And then we'll go and get dressed.

André You see?

Laura What?

André You see? What you just said . . .

Laura Well . . .

André You're speaking to me as if I were retarded.

Laura I'm not.

André You are!

Laura I'm not, I . . .

André 'And then we'll go and get dressed . . .' 'Your little blue pill . . . '

Pause.

Thing is, I'm very intelligent. Very. Sometimes I even surprise myself. You need to bear that in mind, d'you understand?

Laura Yes, I'll . . . bear it in mind.

André Thank you.

Pause.

It's true. I'm very . . . Sometimes I even surprise myself. Memory like an elephant.

Brief pause.

(*Wanting to make himself absolutely clear.*) You know, the animal.

Laura Yes, yes.

He drinks his glass of water without taking his medication.

You've forgotten your pills!

He looks at them in the hollow of his hand.

André Oh, yes, so I did . . . What are they doing there?

Laura I'll go and get you another glass of water.

André No, no. Don't bother. I'll swallow them with the . . .

Laura What?

André You'll see. With the coffee.

Laura Are you sure?

André Positive.

Laura It'd be easier with the . . .

André No, it wouldn't. Look. Here. (*He begins what seems to him the equivalent of a magic trick.*) You'll see.

Are you watching? Watch carefully. I'll stick them in my gob. Watch, there they go, hey presto, they're in my mouth. Did you see? Did you see? Did you see?

Laura Yes, yes. I . . . I'm watching.

André Good. And now, the coffee. Watch carefully . . . Hey presto.

He swallows the pills.

The job is done.

Laura Bravo.

André (*modestly*) I worked in the circus for a bit when I was young.

Laura Did you?

André Yes. I was quite talented. Especially at conjuring tricks. Do you like conjuring tricks? Would you like me to show you a little magic? I need a pack of cards. Do you have one?

Laura No.

André There must be one in one of these drawers . . . We have to find it. Clubs, hearts, diamonds and spades!

He rubs his hands.

I've always liked cards. Before I was married, I often used to play with friends. Sometimes till the small hours of the morning. Hearts and spades. Place your bets! I'm going to show you a trick you've never seen. Clubs! A magic trick, invented by me. You'll see. Or rather, you won't see. You'll be blinded. Blinded!

Laura Let's get dressed first.

André Now?

Laura Yes.

André (*like a child*) Oh, no, not now.

Laura Yes.

André Oh, no.

Laura Yes.

André What's the point? I'll only have to put my pyjamas back on tonight, won't I? Might as well save some time.

Laura I see what you mean. But if you keep your pyjamas on, we won't be able to go out.

André Where did you want to go?

Laura The park. It's a nice day.

Suddenly a Man walks in. He also has a cup of coffee in his hand.

Man Everything going well?

Laura Fine. We were going to get dressed.

André But . . .

Laura Are you coming with me?

André can't understand what this man is doing in his flat.

Man Everything all right, André?

André is rooted to the spot. He doesn't answer.

Something the matter?

André No, no . . .

Man I just wanted a word with you. In fact.

André With me?

Man Yes.

Laura In that case, I'll . . . I'll go and get your things ready.

André (*alarmed*) No, wait a minute . . .

Laura I'll be back.

André Don't leave me on my own.

Laura What? I'll be in the next room. I'll be right back.

Laura exits. We can see André is intimidated, as if this stranger's presence frightened him. Same positions and layout as Scene Five.

Man Can I ask you a question?

André Yes.

The Man moves closer to him. There's something threatening about his approach.

Man But I want an honest answer. Nothing fancy . . . Can you do that for me?

André (*caught off guard*) Yes.

Man Well, then . . .

Brief pause.

How much longer do you intend to hang around getting on everybody's tits?

André Me?

Man Yes, you. I'd like to know your opinion. At least, on this subject. I'm curious to know how much longer you intend to hang around getting on everybody's tits?

Brief pause.

I mean, do you intend to go on ruining your daughter's life? Or is it too much to hope that you'll behave reasonably in the foreseeable future?

André But . . . what are you talking about?

Man About you, André. About you. Your attitude.

He gives him a little slap.

André What are you doing? I can't allow this.

Man You can't allow it?

André No.

Man Suppose I do it again, then what will you do?

André I'll . . .

Man Yes?

André You'll have to take me on. Physically.

Man Are you saying that to tempt me?

Brief pause.

See, me as well, there's something I can't allow. Getting on everybody's tits. Past a certain age.

He smiles and gives him a second little slap.

André Stop it! Do you hear me? Stop this at once.

The Man still has a broad, menacing smile on his face. André, opposite him, looks helpless.

Man Yes. I won't put up with that. I find that totally inappropriate. At your age.

He gives him a third little slap.

André Stop that! I told you to stop it!

Man All right. I'll stop. If you're going to take it like that. But I hope I've made myself clear. That the message has come across. Otherwise, I'm going to have to . . .

André What?

Brief pause.

What?

Man What do you think . . .?

He raises his hand, as if preparing to deliver another slap and André covers his face. For a moment, he's in this humiliating defensive position. Then Anne returns from the kitchen: the follow-on to Scene Five. Mood change. She's carrying the dish with the chicken.

Anne Right. I couldn't find your watch, Dad. We'll have another look later, because now the chicken's ready. We can sit down for dinner.

She sees her father.

Dad. Dad, what's the matter?

Blackout.

ELEVEN

Almost immediately. André and Pierre (in the position of the Man). Anne comes in with the dish in her hands. A repeat.

Anne Right. I couldn't find your watch, Dad. We'll have another look later, because now the chicken's ready. We can sit down for dinner.

She sees her father.

Dad. Dad, what's the matter? (*To Pierre.*) What's the matter with him?

Pierre I don't know.

She puts the dish down and approaches her father, who's maintained the same position, as if afraid of being slapped.

Anne Dad . . . Dad . . . What's the matter? Look at me. Are you all right? What is it?

André I . . .

Anne What's the matter?

André begins to sob.

Is it because of your watch? Dad, is that the reason? We'll find it, I promise you. All right? I promise you. I haven't had the time to do a proper search yet. But we'll find it. All right? Shush. Come on, don't cry.

While she speaks, she's holding him in her arms and stroking his hair. She looks at Pierre with a concerned expression. Then Pierre sits at the table. He pours himself a glass of wine.

You'll be all right now. Mm? Shush . . . You'll be all right. You'll be all right. Let's eat our chicken. Shall we? You like chicken, don't you?

André But what time is it?

Anne It's eight o'clock. Time to eat.

André Eight o'clock in the evening?

Anne Yes, Dad.

André But I thought it was morning. I've only just got up. Look, I'm still in my pyjamas.

Anne No, it's evening and I've cooked you a chicken. Come on, let's eat. Come on. Little daddy. Little daddy.

He seems very lost.

Pause.

Blackout.

TWELVE

The room, a little later. André is already in bed. Pierre and Anne. A repeat.

Anne Any left?

Pierre Yes. Want a glass?

Anne Please.

He gets up and pours one for her.

He was so strange this evening.

Pierre You know what I think.

Anne It's worrying me.

Pierre Shall we change the subject?

Anne Yes. Sorry.

Long pause. Sense of strain.

It's good, this wine.

Pierre Yes.

Pause. They smile at each other. Silence.

Anne I've been thinking about what you said earlier on. About . . . When you said we should put him in a nursing home.

Pierre Oh?

Anne Yes. And I was thinking maybe you were right. Maybe you were right, after all.

Pierre I think I was.

Anne It hurt me so much to see him like that this evening.

Pierre Yes.

Anne I had the feeling he was frightened of you.

Pierre I know.

Anne I'm frightened of you too.

Pause. Oddly, he smiles.

Pierre Don't talk such nonsense. Stop being frightened. Believe me, this is the right decision. Afterwards, we'll be able to lighten up a little. Go away somewhere. Wouldn't you like to go away?

Anne Where?

Pierre I don't know. A long way away. Just the two of us. Live a bit . . .

Brief pause.

Listen to me, you have no reason to feel guilty. It doesn't make any sense.

Anne Sense? What does make any sense?

Pierre Being happy. Being together. Being alive.

She kisses him.

Blackout.

THIRTEEN

The following morning. By now the flat is practically empty. André is alone. Suddenly, Anne appears.

Anne Up already?

André I didn't sleep.

Anne Last night?

André No. Not a wink.

Anne Why? Aren't you feeling well?

André Have you seen?

Anne What?

André What do you mean, 'What?' Look around you. There's no furniture.

Anne So?

André So? We've been burgled.

Anne No, we haven't.

André But you can see, there's nothing here!

Anne It's always been like this, Dad. It's the way the flat is designed.

André Is that what you think?

Anne Of course. It's always been like this.

André I'm sorry, you're wrong.

Anne I'm not. I don't think. Don't you like it? You think it's a bit minimal?

André Horrible, more like. Who's done this? Who designed it?

Anne I did, Dad.

André Did you? But there's nothing here.

Anne I know. I like it like that. Right. I need a coffee. How about you?

André There was furniture. I remember it. There were pieces of furniture all over the place.

Anne You're mixing it up with your flat, Dad. It's always been like this here. Right. I'm going to have a coffee. Then, we'll get dressed.

She exits.

André Already?

Anne (*off*) Yes. You have a visitor today. Remember?

Pause.

(*Off.*) Dad, do you remember?

André My dear, you must give up this habit of repeating the same thing over and over again, it gets very boring. Burble, burble, burble. Never-ending burbling on. Of course I remember. How could I have forgotten? You never stop talking about it.

Anne has returned.

Anne I'm sorry. I just wanted to be sure you'd remembered. She shouldn't be long.

André This early?

Anne Yes. She's supposed to come for your breakfast. Would you like a coffee before she . . .?

André I dreamt about her last night.

Anne Laura?

André Yes. Well, I think I did. I can see her face.

Anne smiles at him.

You know, she really reminded me of your sister . . .

Anne Laura? Yes. That's what you said yesterday.

André Doesn't she remind you?

Anne Mm? Yes, perhaps.

Pause.

Anyway, if you like her, I'm happy. She seems really nice. I mean, sweet. And efficient. She'll look after you well.

André Yes. I like her.

Anne Good. We'd better get you dressed before she arrives, don't you think?

André Who?

Anne Laura. Your new carer. The one you like.

André Ah, yes, yes, yes.

Anne Better to have a jacket on when she arrives.

André And trousers.

Anne She very much enjoyed meeting you yesterday, you know. She found you very . . .

André Very what?

Anne I can't remember the word she used . . . Oh, yes. Charming. She said you were charming.

André Did she?

Anne I must say, you did quite a little number on her.

André I did?

Anne Yes. You convinced her you knew how to dance. That you were good at tap dancing.

André Me?

Anne (*laughing*) Yes.

André (*a childlike smile*) And what did she say?

Anne She said she hoped you'd give her a demonstration. One day.

André Funny. I didn't even know I knew how to tap dance. Did you?

Anne No.

André Hidden talents.

Anne Apparently, yes.

André Tap dancing?

Brief pause. He reflects. Doorbell.

Anne Ah.

André Is that her?

Anne I expect so.

André But . . . so soon? I'm not ready. I'm not dressed.

Anne Never mind. You can get dressed later.

André No. I . . . I have to put some trousers on, Anne. Anne, I'm not properly dressed.

Anne It doesn't matter.

Anne is heading for the door.

André Yes, it does matter.

Anne You can get dressed later. She's outside the door.

André Anne.

Anne What?

André Don't leave me like this. I'm not properly dressed. What's she going to think of me? I have to get dressed. Where are my clothes?

Anne Dad. Why do you always make everything so difficult? You can get dressed later. There's nothing to worry about.

André I'll be mortified . . .

Anne No, you won't.

André I will. Look, I'm in my pyjamas. I have to put my trousers on.

The doorbell rings again. Anne opens the door. It's the Woman who appears.

Anne Hello.

Woman Hello. Not too late, am I?

Anne No, no. Not at all. Come in. Come in.

The Woman comes in.

Woman Thank you.

André But . . . who is this?

Anne We were expecting you. Come in. Thanks for coming so early.

André But, Anne . . . It's not her.

Anne Dad. (*To the Woman.*) Would you like something to drink? Coffee?

Woman No, thanks.

Anne Have you had breakfast? Make yourself comfortable. I . . .

André I don't want her. Where's the one I like? Where is she?

Anne But Dad . . . What are you talking about? Say hello to Laura.

André There's something that doesn't make sense about this. It doesn't make sense!

Pause.

Woman Do you remember me? We met yesterday.

Pause.

We were starting to get to know one another . . .

Pause. André seems panicked. He takes a step backwards.

And I told you I'd come back . . . Just to see the way you did things and whether I could help you . . .

Pause.

D'you remember?

Pause.

You don't remember?

Pause.

André? D'you remember?

Pause.

D'you remember?

Pause.

Blackout.

FOURTEEN

Almost immediately. No more furniture. The Woman is there.

Anne I need to talk to you, Dad.

Pause. André looks frightened.

I've spoken to Pierre.

André Pierre?

Anne Pierre, Dad. I've spoken to him.

André I don't care for him, that fellow.

Anne He's not a fellow, Dad. He's the man I love.

Pause.

Anyway, I've spoken to him and . . . You remember, at first, when you came . . . How shall I put this? I'm wondering if it wouldn't be better to . . . What do you think of this room?

Brief pause.

Mm? It's rather nice, isn't it?

Woman It looks on to the park.

Anne Yes. It's very nice. It's like being in a hotel. Don't you think?

Woman That's what all the residents say.

Anne I think you might be better off here.

André Where?

Anne Here. I was wondering if it wouldn't be more reassuring . . . nicer for you if we came to a joint decision that you should move in here.

Brief pause.

What do you think?

André What about you? What are you going to do? Where are you going to sleep? Which room?

Anne If you remember, I'm going to go and live in London.

André No, you're not.

Anne I am. Remember? I told you about it . . . Remember?

André But you said . . . Are you sure?

Anne Yes.

André You told me you were staying here with me . . .

Anne No, I have to go. It's important. I already explained it to you. But I'll come and see you. Occasional weekends.

André What about me?

Anne You'll stay here. In Paris.

André All on my own?

Pause.

What about your sister? Where's she?

Anne Dad . . .

André What?

Pause.

If you knew how much I missed her . . .

Anne I do too, Dad, I miss her too. We all miss her.

André takes a look at her, makes a gesture, perhaps even caresses her, as if for once he understood what can't be spoken.

Pause.

Blackout.

FIFTEEN

A white bed, reminiscent of a hospital bed. André doesn't know where he is. Then the Woman comes in. She's wearing a white coat.

Woman Did you sleep well?

André What am I doing here?

Woman It's time.

André I didn't ask about the time. I asked what I was doing here.

Woman How do you mean?

André Who put this bed here? In the middle of the drawing room? Anne? This is really getting out of hand. I'm sorry to say this, but it is getting out of hand.

Woman Don't get upset.

André I'm not upset. I'm just saying you don't put a bed in the middle of a drawing room. It doesn't make any sense at all. Where's Anne?

Woman Look, I've brought you your medication.

André Why don't you bugger off with your medication! What are you, a nurse?

Woman Yes.

André (*finally realising who he's talking to*) Oh, you are . . . Oh, so that's it . . . Oh, I see. You're a nurse . . .

Woman Yes.

André Oh, I see. That's what I was thinking. You're the type. Typical nurse. So what are you doing here?

Woman Sorry?

André What are you doing here?

Woman Looking after you.

André You don't say! Looking after me?

Woman Yes.

André First I've heard of it. Since when?

Woman For quite a few weeks now.

André For quite a few weeks? I'm happy to hear it. Amazing! Nobody tells me anything in this house. It's always a *fait accompli*. I really need a little word with Anne. We can't go on like this. It's really starting to . . . But I thought we were getting a new one.

Woman A new what?

André Nurse. A new nurse.

Pause.

The one who looked a bit like Elise. My other daughter.

Brief pause.

I met her the other day. Didn't I?

Woman All right. Will you take your medication?

André She was supposed to start this morning. Laura. Wasn't she?

Woman I think you're getting mixed up, André.

André The one who reminded me of Elise . . .

Woman (*impatiently*) Right.

André Yes, all right, fine. Let's take this medication. It's not timed to the minute, is it?

Pause. He takes his time.

What time is it?

Woman Time for your medication.

André I've lost my watch. You don't know where . . .? I've lost my watch . . . Anne? Anne?

Woman Your daughter isn't here, André.

André Oh? Where is she? Has she gone out?

Woman If you remember, your daughter lives in London.

André What? No, she thought about going. But in the end, it didn't happen.

Woman She's been living there several months.

André My daughter? In London? No, listen, it never stops raining in London.

Woman Look, yesterday, this postcard she sent you, we read it together. Don't you remember?

André What is this nonsense?

Woman Look.

She shows him a postcard. He reads it.

I tell you this every day. You ought to remember it by now. She lives in London because she met a man called Pierre, who she now lives with. But she comes to see you sometimes.

André Anne?

Woman Yes. Occasionally she comes for the weekend. She comes here. You go for a walk in the park. She tells you about her new life, what she's up to. The other day, she brought you some tea. Because you like tea.

André Me? I detest tea. I only drink coffee.

Woman But it's very good tea.

The Man comes in. He's also dressed in white.

Man Everything all right?

Woman Fine. We were just going to get dressed.

Man Everything all right?

André doesn't answer. The Man hands a document to the Woman, which she signs.

Woman There you are.

Man Thanks. Have a nice day.

Woman See you later.

André Him, this one . . . Who is he?

The Man exits.

Woman Who?

André Him . . . Who just left.

Woman That's Olivier.

André Olivier?

Woman Yes.

André Are you sure?

Woman Yes. Why?

André Nothing. But . . . How shall I put this? What's he doing here? I mean . . . in my flat. Do I know him?

Woman Yes. He's Olivier. You see him every day.

André Do I? And you . . .

Woman What?

André Sorry to ask this, but my mind's gone blank . . . I mean, you . . . you . . . Who are you, exactly?

Woman I'm Martine.

André Martine. That's right. Yes, yes, yes. Martine. And he's Olivier.

Woman Yes.

André Right. Right. And . . . What about me?

Woman What about you?

André Me . . . Who exactly am I?

Woman You? You're André.

André André?

Woman Yes.

André Are you sure?

Woman (*amused*) Yes.

André André? Nice name, André . . . Don't you think?

Woman It's a very nice name.

André My mother gave it to me. I imagine. Did you know her?

Woman Who?

André My mother.

Woman No.

André She was so . . . She had very big eyes. It was . . . I can see her face now. I hope she'll come and see me sometimes. Mummy. Do you think? You were saying she might come occasionally for the weekend . . .

Woman Your daughter?

He's crushed by sudden grief.

André No, Mummy. I . . . I want my mummy. I want my mummy. I want . . . I want to get out of here. Have someone come and fetch me.

Woman Now. Shush . . .

André I want my mummy. I want her to come and fetch me. I want to go back home.

André starts sobbing. The Woman is surprised: she hadn't in any way anticipated this grief.

Woman But . . . What's the matter with you? André . . . André . . . What's the matter with you? Come here. Come to me . . . Tell me what the matter is . . .

André I . . .

Woman Yes?

André I feel as if . . . I feel as if I'm losing all my leaves, one after another.

Woman Your leaves? What are you talking about?

André The branches! And the wind . . . I don't understand what's happening any more. Do you understand what's happening? All this business about the flat? You don't know where you can put your head down any more. I know where my watch is. On my wrist. That I do know. For the journey. If not, I wouldn't know when I might have to . . .

Woman First, we'll get dressed, shall we?

André Yes.

Woman We'll get dressed and then we'll go and have a walk in the park. All right?

André Yes.

Woman Good. All the trees. And the leaves. And then we'll come back here and have something to eat. In the refectory. Then you'll have a siesta. All right? And if you're on form, we'll take another little walk. In the park. The two of us. Because it's a nice day. Isn't it?

André Yes.

Woman The sun's out. We have to make the most of it. It doesn't happen every day. It never lasts very long when the weather's as good as this, does it? So let's go and get dressed, is that all right?

He clings on to her.

André No.

Woman Now. Don't be a baby. Come on. Come with me. All right? Come on. Easy. Easy. Shush. Shush. You'll be all right in a minute. You'll be all right. Shush . . .

He calms down, buried in her arms. She rocks him gently.

Pause.

Blackout.